Editor: Catherine Bradley
Art Director: Charles Matheson
Designer: Malcolm Smythe
Researcher: Cecilia Weston-Baker

Illustrated by Ron Hayward
Associates and Peter Bull

© Aladdin Books Ltd

Designed and produced by
Aladdin Books Ltd
70 Old Compton Street
London W1V 5PA

First published in the
United States in 1986 by
Franklin Watts
387 Park Avenue South
New York NY 10016

ISBN 0-531-10233-5

Printed in Belgium

Library of Congress
Catalog Card No. 86-50274

CONFLICT IN THE 20th CENTURY

THE RISE OF THE DICTATORS

1919–1939

PETER BANYARD

Edited by Dr John Pimlott

FRANKLIN WATTS

New York · London · Toronto · Sydney

INTRODUCTION

The period 1919-39 was one of immense political change, particularly in Europe. Once the horror of the First World War had ended, the victorious powers – principally Britain, France, Italy and the United States – vowed to produce a settlement that would prevent a repetition of such conflict. Germany, Austria-Hungary, Bulgaria and Turkey were all forced to accept peace terms that involved loss of territory, restrictions on economic and military strength and the payment of compensation to the victors. New states – Yugoslavia, Czechoslovakia and a re-formed Poland – were created, to act as "buffers" between the more powerful countries of Europe, as well as to satisfy growing nationalist demands. A special League of Nations was established to act as mediator in future crises.

Dreams of a future free from war proved false. Among the defeated powers, resentment grew as the full scale of the peace terms became apparent and the economic impact of the four years of war began to bite. By the early 1930s, the world was in the grip of an economic "depression" that was to produce widespread unemployment and poverty.

It was out of these circumstances that a number of dictators – harsh men offering harsh solutions – emerged. The process had begun as early as 1922, when the Fascist leader, Benito Mussolini, gained power in Italy. His example was followed in Germany, where the Nazi leader Adolf Hitler came to power in 1933. In Spain, Francisco Franco emerged victorious from the Civil War of 1936-39. Not all the dictators were right-wing; by the late 1920s Stalin had established a firm hold over Communist Soviet Russia.

In all cases, however, the dictators created pressures on the peace settlement hammered out in 1919 and, in the face of US isolationism and continued Anglo-French weakness, little could be done to prevent its gradual destruction. By the late 1930s, with both Italy and Germany intent on expansion and the League of Nations powerless to prevent it, conflict became inevitable. The peacemakers of 1919 had failed and the world plunged once more into the nightmare of war.

DR JOHN PIMLOTT *Series Editor*

EDITORIAL PANEL

Series Editor:
Dr John Pimlott, Senior Lecturer in the Department of War Studies and International Affairs, RMA Sandhurst, U.K.

Editorial Advisory Panel:
Brigadier General James L Collins Jr, US Army Chief of Military History 1970–82

General Sir John Hackett, former Commander-in-Chief of the British Army of the Rhine and Principal of King's College, London, U.K.

Ian Hogg, retired Master Gunner of the Artillery, British Army and editor of *Jane's Infantry Weapons*

John Keegan, Senior Lecturer in the Department of War Studies and International Affairs, RMA Sandhurst, U.K.

Professor Laurence Martin, Vice-Chancellor of the University of Newcastle-upon-Tyne, U.K.

Members of the elite Leibstandarte Adolf Hitler *SS unit, Hitler's personal guard, goose step past during a parade to celebrate Hitler's birthday, April 20, 1938. The swastika symbol was used by the Nazis on their flags and badges. Although it originated in India, it had been used by the Teutonic tribes in Germany since the 5th century.*

CONTENTS

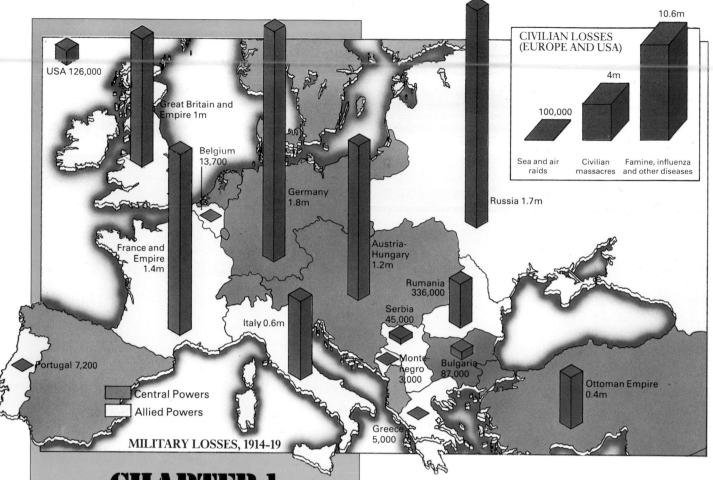

USA 126,000

Great Britain and Empire 1m

Belgium 13,700

Germany 1.8m

France and Empire 1.4m

Russia 1.7m

Austria-Hungary 1.2m

Rumania 336,000

Serbia 45,000

Italy 0.6m

Portugal 7,200

Monte-negro 3,000

Bulgaria 87,000

Ottoman Empire 0.4m

Greece 5,000

CIVILIAN LOSSES (EUROPE AND USA)

10.6m

4m

100,000

| Sea and air raids | Civilian massacres | Famine, influenza and other diseases |

Central Powers
Allied Powers

MILITARY LOSSES, 1914-19

CHAPTER 1
THE AFTERMATH OF WAR

Europe suffered enormously in the First World War. Britain and France had been through years of effort and loss on an unprecedented scale and were determined that this should not be forgotten or thrown away. To this end, France was determined to make the Germans pay for the damage they had done and, with a smaller population and less resources than Germany, it wanted to keep Germany weak. The German people, however, could not accept the harsh terms imposed on them by the victors. The concern of Britain, which was now exhausted and poor, was to avoid another general war. Russia went from the First World War to revolution and civil war. It was about to embark on the economic and social transformation that would make it a great power. The only power to emerge from the conflict in a strong position was the United States, but it was so sickened by the foreign quarrels that it withdrew into isolation.

As early as September 29, 1918, the top German generals advised Kaiser Wilhelm II that Germany should seek an armistice. The generals, Hindenburg and Ludendorff, were admitting that Germany could not win the war. Rumors of defeat spread and created massive unrest among the armed forces and the German people. Against this background, the new German civilian government negotiated with the Allies knowing there was no choice, and agreed to an armistice. On November 11 the guns stopped firing on the Western Front. After four years of fighting all was quiet.

The "Big Three" impose their terms

It cannot be denied that some of the Allied leaders were out for revenge as they hammered out the details of the peace settlement. They had to take into account the feelings of France and Britain – two countries that had suffered shocking casualties and financial loss in the recent war. After a war in which nearly 1.4 million soldiers from France and its empire had died and vast debts had been built up, the French Prime Minister, Georges Clemenceau, was keen to express the vengeful sentiments of his people.

Clemenceau had always urged military readiness to meet the German threat. It was obvious enough to him that roughly 40 million Frenchmen were unlikely to win a future war against some 65 million Germans. He was determined that Germany would never again be strong enough to threaten French frontiers. He was the main instigator of a demand for a demilitarized buffer zone (an area where there would be no military forces) between the two countries, as well as a limitation of German armed forces. At the peace conference he also insisted on financial compensation, known as reparations, to help pay French debts to Britain and to the United States.

The British Prime Minister, David Lloyd George, had just won the December 1918 election on the slogan "Make Germany Pay," but he was too wise a politician to harbor anti-German sentiments himself. Despite this, he could not ignore the mood of the British people and was determined to serve British national interests. There were 761,000 British dead to mourn and a debt of some $4.3 billion to the United States. This debt was a matter of great significance because it was a contributing factor to Britain's decline from being the world's greatest power.

Alongside France and Britain, the United States was one of the "Big Three" powers which had the most influence on the eventual settlement. President Woodrow Wilson was far more high-minded and disinterested than his allies. America had spent the greater part of the war as a neutral power, and although the Americans had entered the war in April 1917, they had no national interests at stake in Europe. Indeed, the war and its aftermath became increasingly unpopular with the American people.

In the November 1918 elections, the Democratic Party had lost its majority in both the Senate and the House of Representatives. This undermined Wilson's position at the peace conference, which was unfortunate because he had long shown a determination to achieve a just and lasting peace.

The peace treaties

The Big Three leaders and their advisors began to arrive in Paris for the peace conference in December 1918. They were joined by delegations from 24 other, lesser powers, only two of which – Italy and Japan – were to play significant roles. Both were concerned to make territorial gains at the expense of the defeated countries and both enjoyed some success.

By the end of 1919, Italy had gained possession of territory from Austria, but had been forced to abandon claims to Dalmatia (now part of Yugoslavia) and had been prevented by the Big Three from gaining the port of Fiume. Japan experienced similar pressures, for although it took possession of former German islands in the North Pacific, its claims to permanent rule over the Chinese ports of Tsingtao and Shantung were effectively blocked by President Wilson. This meant that both Italy and Japan were dissatisfied with the rewards of the recent struggle.

David Lloyd George leaves the Palace of Versailles, after signing the peace treaty on June 28, 1919.

Germany signs the Treaty of Versailles

After six months of delay, the German delegation was presented with the treaty at Versailles, near Paris, in May 1919 and given 15 days to consider it. The delegates were not the representatives of the old order that had ruled Germany throughout the war, but of a new, uncertain, democratic state that existed precariously. Under the Kaiser, political parties had enjoyed little real power; the war had been directed by the Kaiser and increasingly by his generals.

The political and social unrest in November 1918 had forced the Kaiser to abdicate and his Chancellor to resign. The Social Democrat Party, led by Friedrich Ebert, took over the government. Germany's first real democratic elections were held on January 19, 1919 and the Social Democrats won a majority of the votes.

Even before these elections, there had been a Communist uprising in Berlin, known as the Spartacist Revolt, led by Karl Liebknecht and Rosa Luxemburg. From January 5 to 11, 1919 the city was in chaos, with bitter street fighting between Spartacist gangs and members of the *Freikorps*, independent paramilitary units raised by right-wing, ex-army officers. Both Liebknecht and Luxemburg were captured, only to be shot while "trying to escape," and the revolt was brutally suppressed by the *Freikorps*. The role of the *Freikorps* showed how weak Ebert's government was. To political weakness was added military defenselessness, because the armistice terms had effectively deprived Germany of forces capable of defending it against the 39 Allied divisions still in existence and poised on the German border.

The delegation had no choice but to accept the terms dictated by the Allies, although they made a brave but futile attempt to reject the most odious clause of all – the one which insisted that Germany alone was guilty of provoking the war. All protests were rejected and, on June 28, the Germans signed the Treaty in the Hall of Mirrors at Versailles.

The Treaty itself was derived from the Fourteen Points presented by President Wilson to Congress in January 1918, although these had been revised during the peace conference, making the terms much harsher on Germany.

The League of Nations

The Treaty itself was a mixture of hopeful sentiment and territorial detail. Under hopeful sentiment came clauses banning secret treaties, demanding arms reduction throughout the world and setting up a League of Nations to preserve the peace in future. A covenant which set out the aims and organization of the League was incorporated into each of the peace treaties, imposed on Germany, Austria, Hungary, Bulgaria and Turkey. Signatories of the peace treaties (but not the defeated nations) became members of the League.

Revolutionary sailors and civilians take up arms and occupy a castle in Berlin, November 1918.

Freikorps units terrorize the population in Berlin during the Spartacist Rising in January 1919.

Other "neutral" countries were invited to join and a total of 42 states originally sent representatives to the League's Assembly in Geneva. Any member state which ignored its obligations under the Covenant and resorted to war was considered to have committed aggression against all the other League members and economic "sanctions" or penalties would be imposed on the offending country.

Above the Assembly was a Council of five permanent members (originally intended to be the United States, France, Britain, Italy and Japan) and four non-permanent members elected by the Assembly. The Council could recommend military action to end a war along the lines of "collective security" (concerted action by the forces of the member states.)

President Wilson had come up with the idea of the League but it was enthusiastically accepted by the other Allies – particularly Britain – which hoped that it would help to remove the threat of a future general war. Unfortunately the United States never became a member. President Wilson's involvement in European affairs was very unpopular. The politicians followed public opinion and the Senate rejected the Versailles Treaty twice. The United States gradually withdrew from the European peace settlement and retreated into isolation. The US absence meant the Council lacked the power it so urgently needed.

The terms of the Versailles Treaty

Under territorial detail came a number of changes, in which Germany lost 13 per cent of its territory. France regained Alsace-Lorraine, lost in the Franco-Prussian War of 1870-71. The Saar territory in western Germany was to be administered by an International Commission for 15 years and the production of its coalfields was awarded to France as compensation for the ruin of French coalfields in the northeast by Germany during the war.

At the end of the 15 years there was to be a plebiscite to decide the future of the Saar. A plebiscite is an election, held on a single issue, to find out the people's wishes. As it happened, the population decided to reunite with Germany when this was held in 1935. Germany also lost three small areas to Belgium while, to the north, the border with Denmark was adjusted by a plebiscite in which northern Schleswig voted to become Danish.

Worse was to come in the east. It was part of the Allies' concern that the various ethnic groups of Europe should gain their independence in new nation states. It was also considered worthwhile to create buffer states between the three great land powers of Russia, Germany and France, preventing direct territorial clashes and containing Germany within a net of smaller states.

In the east it was possible to put the new states of Poland and Czechoslovakia between Germany and Russia. However, it was felt that Poland could not function properly as an independent state without access to the sea, and this could only be gained at German expense. To create the new Polish state, Germany was forced to transfer to it Posen, West Prussia and part of Upper Silesia. To give Poland access to the sea, the German port of Danzig was made a free city, administered by the League of Nations but with Poland enjoying special rights there. At the same time, a stretch of land to the west of Danzig gave Poland unrestricted access to the sea and enabled the Poles to build their own port at Gdynia (Gdansk).

German resentment at the loss of predominantly German-speaking areas was profound, but the Polish buffer state was now a reality. There was no such latitude to the west as there was no non-German group on the western border of Germany which could be used to establish a buffer.

Instead the Rhineland was to be demilitarized and no troops or weapons deployed anywhere between the German border and a line 50 km (31 miles) to the east. As a further sop to French fears of German military resurgence, the German army was to be limited to a total of 100,000 men, the General Staff was to be abolished and military aircraft were prohibited. To reduce British fears about Germany's naval power, the new German Navy was severely limited. No submarines were to be built, and the entire German armaments industry was to be controlled and inspected.

The Allies also stripped Germany of her colonies. In Africa, Britain took over Tanganyika and shared both Togoland and The Cameroons with France, while the Union of South Africa received German South West Africa. Elsewhere, former German islands in the Pacific north of the Equator went to Japan and those to the south were shared between Australia and New Zealand.

In all cases, the new territories were to be mandates under the authority of the emergent League of Nations. A mandated territory was a colonial possession in all but name, but it was supposed to be administered by the mandatory power for the benefit of its people until they were capable of self-government.

The legacy of Versailles

There was much in all these arrangements that was to cause problems in years to come. The tiny German Army, for instance, was too small to contain the violent political disorder which made the new, democratic Germany unstable. However, if there was a single issue that soured the relations between victors and vanquished, it was the matter of reparations. The Allies had forced the German delegation to accept guilt for the war and it then followed that Germany must make financial reparations to those who had suffered.

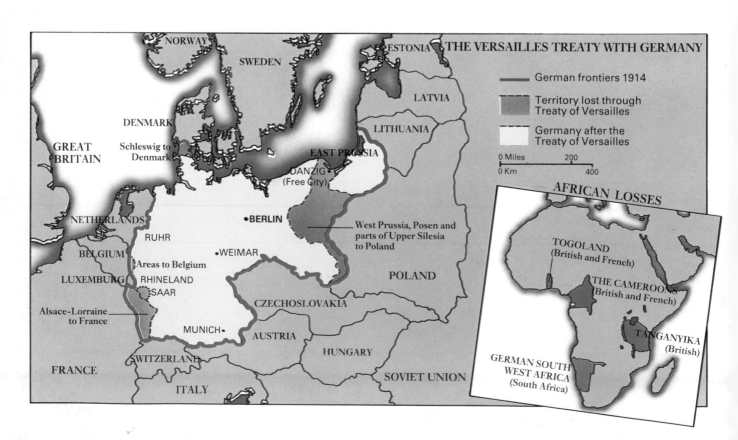

Basically the war had enriched America but impoverished the other Allies, which were in debt to the United States. Britain owed almost $5 billion and France owed over $4 billion. The US refused to waive these war debts, so the debtor countries became determined to squeeze at least part of them out of their defeated enemy. A figure of $33 billion (132 billion gold marks) was arrived at in a fairly arbitrary manner and demanded from the Germans, to be paid in full by May 1, 1921.

The great economist John Maynard Keynes, who was advising the British delegation at the conference, warned them that the Germans could not pay this and urged the Allies to accept a more modest $11 billion (44 billion gold marks). Indeed, Keynes had the strongest reservations about the value of any reparations, chiefly because Germany could only earn the necessary foreign currency by massive exports, which would cause unemployment in the receiving countries. He was right: the payments proved too great and were never fully made before the idea was eventually scrapped in 1932.

The Kapp Putsch

The Versailles Treaty was much harsher than the German people had expected. They refused to believe the German Army had been defeated in the field and consequently were quick to blame the politicians. The new German government was named the Weimar Republic, after the German town in which the new constitution had been drawn up, and its authority was immediately undermined by the fact that it accepted the Treaty terms. There was, of course, no question of putting up any physical resistance to the Allies' overwhelming military power.

In March 1920, elements of the *Freikorps* mounted a counterrevolution, led by Wolfgang Kapp and General Walther von Lüttwitz, the so-called "Kapp Putsch," and occupied Berlin. The elected government and national assembly fled. The German Army refused to come to the aid of the government and the putsch was only defeated by a general strike of German workers. Kapp and von Lüttwitz fled into exile, but it was apparent that the Weimar government had little real authority in Germany.

Freikorps supporters of the Kapp Putsch taking a lunch break in Berlin, March 1920.

The treaty with Austria

The peace terms had seemed harsh enough to Germany, but they were even worse for her allies. In his wish to establish a just and lasting peace, President Wilson put forward the principle of self-determination for the diverse peoples of Europe. The other Allies generally accepted this because the incident which had sparked off the First World War – the assassination of Archduke Francis Ferdinand at Sarajevo in June 1914 – seemed to have been a result of frustrated nationalism.

Because of the mixture of nationalities in central and eastern Europe, it was impossible to define borders to create new states without including sizable ethnic minorities – a group of people sharing a language and culture – within them. Nevertheless the Allies split the Austro-Hungarian Empire into rough national groupings. Wherever there was a questionable issue, it was resolved to the disadvantage of Austria and Hungary – the old kingdoms of the Empire.

Austria's turn came at the Treaty of Saint Germain which was imposed on September 10, 1919. Bohemia, Moravia, Austrian Silesia and parts of Lower Austria were given to the new state of Czechoslovakia. Galicia went to Poland and Bukovina was successfully claimed by Rumania, which had come into the war on the Allied side in 1916, only to be swiftly defeated. Another ally, Italy, was rewarded with the South Tyrol (which contained nearly 250,000 Austrians) as well as Trieste and Istria.

Some 4 million German-speaking Austrians became the subjects of other nations and the resulting state of Austria had a population of only 6.5 million, of which 2 million lived in Vienna. What was left could hardly be considered an economic unit. On top of this it had a bill for reparations and was forbidden to unite with Germany. The Austrian Army was limited to 30,000 men and put under the same restrictions as the German armed forces.

The treaty with Hungary

Hungary suffered a similar fate on June 4, 1920 at the Treaty of Trianon. The Hungarians had been through great political upheaval since the end of the war. An attempt to introduce a democracy – a system in which the government is freely elected by the people – had been thwarted by a successful Communist revolution led by Bela Kun in March 1919. The new regime did not last long and was violently overthrown by a right-wing government. In March 1920, Admiral Miklos Horthy became virtual dictator of Hungary and it was his government that was presented with the Allies' terms. He discovered that these were extraordinarily harsh.

Hungary was the chief victim of the Allied policy establishing new states on the principle of self-determination. Large parts of Hungary were given as a reward to some of the lesser Allies, or their successors, for their efforts in the war. Rumania, Yugoslavia and Czechoslovakia took two-thirds of Hungarian territory between them and the Hungarian population was reduced from 18 to 7 million. Besides this the Hungarian Army was restricted to 35,000 volunteers.

The treaty with Bulgaria

Meanwhile, as the last of the defeated European powers, Bulgaria had also been punished at the Treaty of Neuilly, signed on November 27, 1919. During the war, Greece had been on the side of the Allies and was rewarded with western Thrace, while Rumania took Southern Dobruja. The Bulgarian Army was limited to 20,000 men and reparations were demanded. Bulgaria joined the ranks of nations only too anxious to destroy the postwar settlement.

THE TREATIES WITH AUSTRIA-HUNGARY AND BULGARIA

BELGIUM · GERMANY · POLAND · SOVIET UNION · BOHEMIA · SILESIA · Galicia to Poland · CZECHOSLOVAKIA · MORAVIA · SLOVAKIA · RUTHENIA · BUKOVINA · VIENNA · AUSTRIA · HUNGARY · SWITZERLAND · SLOVENIA · To Rumania · FRANCE · South Tyrol to Italy · CROATIA · RUMANIA · Southern Dobruja to Rumania · To Yugoslavia · SERBIA · Istria and Trieste to Italy · DALMATIA · YUGOSLAVIA · BULGARIA · BOSNIA · HERZEGOVINA · SOFIA · MONTENEGRO · TURKEY · ALBANIA · MACEDONIA · Western Thrace to Greece · GREECE

Austro-Hungarian frontiers 1914
Bulgarian frontiers 1914
Territory lost by Austria-Hungary and Bulgaria
Reduced Austria-Hungary and Bulgaria

0 Miles 400
0 Km 200

The new states

Three new states – Yugoslavia, Czechoslovakia and Poland – were created by these treaties. All were a complicated mixture of nationalities, but none more so than Yugoslavia. Centered on the old states of Serbia and Montenegro, it gained Slovenia, Dalmatia and Croatia from the Austro-Hungarian Empire, as well as Bosnia, Herzegovina and Macedonia. At least it made the Balkans look less fragmented on the map, but unfortunately there was a lot of friction among the many different ethnic groups.

The creation of Czechoslovakia was another exercise in putting together different peoples in an attempt to make a sizable country. Czech nationalism had a long tradition and the Czechs had sent a delegation to the Paris Peace Conference to present their case. With their willing cooperation, they were joined by the Slovaks, some 600,000 Ruthenians, 700,000 Hungarians and some 3,250,000 resentful Germans to form a new state powerful enough to restrain Germany in the southeast. In the end, it was this racial diversity that was to prove fatal.

Poland, the largest of the new creations, had previously been an independent state until the end of the 18th century. Despite this, it was hard to settle on acceptable boundaries for a reconstituted Poland. The Allies had decided on an eastern border, which went through lands in which there was a mixture of Poles, Lithuanians, Ukrainians, Russians, Germans and others. Any of these groups could have provided a local ethnic majority.

The Polish head of state, Josef Pilsudski, was a radical politician and soldier whose own birthplace and home town lay to the east of Poland's postwar boundaries in Lithuania. He decided to revise Poland's eastern frontier by force, exploiting the fact that, at the time, Russia was desperately weakened by civil war.

Marshal Josef Pilsudski, Poland's leader

Hungarian Communists demonstrate against the government in October 1918, at the end of the war.

The Russian Revolution and Civil War

In November 1917, the Communist Bolshevik party, led by Lenin, seized power in Russia. The Communists believed in the ideal of a classless society based on the common ownership of industry and property. The revolution had not been accepted throughout the state and civil war broke out when Lenin made peace with Germany in March 1918. Opposition arose from Russian democrats, socialist factions, landowners and supporters of the deposed Tsar – a disparate group, generally described as the "Whites." The Communists were referred to as the "Reds."

By early 1919 the Tsarist Admiral Kolchak had managed to set up a White government in Siberia, while General Denikin raised an army in the Caucasus and General Yudenich led troops based in Estonia.

Some 40,000 Czech soldiers, who had fought for the Russians in the First World War, seized the Trans-Siberian Railway. Meanwhile, troops from the United States, Japan, France and Britain – representing the Western Powers, to whom the anti-democratic nature of Communism was of deep concern – landed in the Caucasus, as well as at Archangel, Murmansk and Vladivostok.

This coalition of enemies should have ensured the overthrow of the Reds, but the foreign powers were only prepared to make a token gesture, while the Czechs were only interested in getting home. In addition, Kolchak, Denikin and Yudenich were indifferent commanders of undisciplined soldiers and followed no common strategy. By comparison, Lev Trotsky, the Red Army's war commissar, was an organizing genius who created a disciplined force.

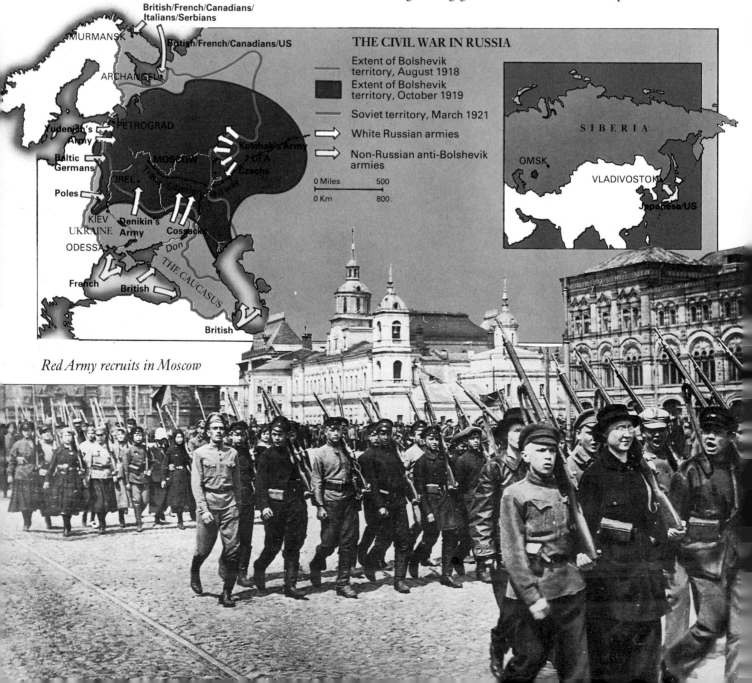

Red Army recruits in Moscow

Japanese troops display the bodies of Communists in Vladivostok, 1920.

The Red Army also had the advantage of holding the most important part of Russia – the west – and had better lines of communication. During 1919 it managed to take on and defeat its White enemies one by one – Kolchak around Ufa and Omsk, Denikin at Kiev and Orel, and Yudenich on the very outskirts of the capital, Petrograd. Overall victory was achieved in early 1920, by which time the foreign powers had withdrawn.

However, the Civil War was devastating, with appalling casualties on both sides. Untold millions of Russians died, not just in military actions, but also of starvation and disease.

The Russo-Polish War

Pilsudski saw in Russia's weakness an opportunity to roll Poland's eastern border forward. In April 1920 he ordered his army to attack and, in the face of only light resistance, advanced deep into Western Russia. The rights and wrongs of this Polish land grab are not easily established. There was no absolute Polish majority in the new territory, but there was some sort of Polish presence throughout it and, in some places, the Polish community was the largest one among a number of diverse races.

Pilsudski could fairly claim that the Polish community was badly and oppressively governed, on the grounds that Russia had been shaken by civil war and was ruled by unelected communists. This was the first direct challenge to the Treaty of Versailles, and the Allies had, in theory, a mechanism to prevent this sort of violent resolution of international problems. This was the League of Nations, which had begun its life on January 10, 1920. But the Western Powers were not at all unhappy about any hostile action directed against Russia, the first Communist state.

However, the Red Army was fresh from its triumphs against the anti-Communist forces in the Civil War and soon counterattacked fiercely. Russian cavalry units pushed the Poles back to Warsaw itself. Meanwhile, the governments of Britain and France were so alarmed by the apparent collapse of the Poles before the Red menace that they dispatched a team of advisors under the leadership of French General Maxime Weygand to Warsaw. Events then moved so fast that the Anglo-French mission arrived as the Poles launched a masterly counterstroke. At the cease fire agreed in October 1920, the Poles were able to insist on keeping parts of western Russia.

THE BREAK-UP OF THE TURKISH EMPIRE

Map key:
- Turkey
- Greek occupation 1919-21
- French Mandates
- British Possessions and Mandates

0 Miles 200
0 Km 400

The treaty with Turkey

Although the Western Allies were not particularly concerned that the Poles had changed the terms of the Versailles Treaty so successfully, they could be expected to take a sterner view of any challenge mounted by a former enemy. Turkey had been the last of the former belligerents to face an imposed peace settlement when Sultan Mohammed VI had agreed to the Treaty of Sèvres in August 1920. Turkey was largely a non-European power. For that reason it was dealt with in a colonial style, with most of its possessions given to Britain and France, while its heartland in Asia Minor was to be divided into zones of European influence. The treaty, however, was never ratified as the Sultan no longer enjoyed effective power.

After its military defeat, Turkey was undergoing a remarkable resurgence. Turkey itself was a reasonably unified state and the Turkish people occupied roughly the area of Asia Minor. From this base the Ottoman Sultans had ruled a huge Middle Eastern Arab empire, which was now given as mandates to Britain and France. Under this system the French were given Greater Syria (out of which they created Lebanon in 1920), while the British took Palestine, Trans-Jordan and Iraq.

The Greek invasion

The Turks seemed prepared to accept the loss of their empire, but when the victorious Allies tried to establish European-ruled areas of Asia Minor – the Turkish heartland – it proved harder to bear. The Italians landed troops at Adalia in 1919 in an attempt to establish an Italian zone of influence when Turkey was partitioned. The Greeks, who had some ancient historical claim to the area of Smyrna, were given Allied support as they occupied eastern Thrace and western Anatolia as far as Izmir. Finally the straits between the Black Sea and the Mediterranean were demilitarized and a small British garrison established at Chanak. With this last move, the Turks effectively lost control of the imperial capital, Constantinople (Istanbul).

Turkish resurgence

A revolt against all this was begun by Mustafa Kemal (Kemal Ataturk), a Turkish general who had distinguished himself in the Gallipoli campaign of 1915. Receiving support from the army and the nationalists in the interior of Turkey, he called for a Grand National Assembly to meet at Ankara in January 1920, openly challenging the Sultan's authority.

Kemal raised an army and the Sultan's forces were defeated at the Battle of Inonu (January 1921). The Italians were wise enough to withdraw from Adalia in June. By September 1921 the Greeks had been forced to retreat, leaving just the British garrison at Chanak. The latter represented a military power that could have defeated Kemal, but the British government declined to become deeply involved. After negotiations, the Chanak force was withdrawn in October 1922, opening the way for a revised settlement of Turkey's frontiers.

On July 24, 1923 the Treaty of Lausanne was signed. In return for Kemal's acceptance of the loss of Turkey's former possessions in the Middle East, the Allies dropped their claims to territory on the Turkish mainland. It was the first negotiated alteration to the peace settlement. This successful outcome boosted Kemal's popularity. Istanbul was restored to Turkish rule, a republic was proclaimed and Kemal was made Turkey's first President.

He did not stop at reasserting national independence. The problem posed by the Greek minority in Anatolia was solved by forcibly deporting the people to Greece. This prompted the Greeks to expel all Turks from their national territory. Some 1.5 million people in all were deported, fueling a Greco-Turkish enmity that was to continue for years.

Kemal now felt free to concentrate on internal reforms. When Kemal died in 1938, Turkey had been transformed from a backward, inefficient Asiatic state into one which looked towards Europe and enjoyed some European standards of government, justice and law. This was a major achievement.

Reparations problems

By the early 1920s, therefore, the peace settlement dictated by the victorious Allies was already dented as a result of violent action by the Poles and the Turks. More destructive still, however, was the German failure to live up to the agreement signed at Versailles. The French felt that the provisions of Versailles were not harsh enough and they reacted swiftly when the Germans began to default on their reparations.

Default occurred in January 1923 and the French retaliated by sending a small force of troops into the Ruhr – Germany's industrial heartland. At the beginning of the year there was an exchange rate of 400 marks to one US dollar. Once the French had occupied the Ruhr to try to force reparations out of Germany in coal, timber and steel, inflation took hold. By August 1923, the new rate was 1,000,000 marks to the dollar and by November 400,000,000.

The situation benefited neither France nor Germany and it was apparent that there should be mediation between the two countries. The world order which the Allied statesmen had hoped to settle at Versailles was already in need of reconstruction. The Germans, of course, favored any move to alter the present situation. They had already ended their diplomatic isolation by concluding a treaty of friendship at Rapallo on April 16, 1922 with another excluded state, communist Russia. It was now obvious that the Western Powers had to accommodate some of Germany's resentments.

The result was a series of treaties and agreements throughout the 1920s, which allowed a gradual renegotiation of Versailles. A start was made with a plan proposed by an American banker, Charles G. Dawes, which was effective from September 1, 1924. It reduced reparations in Germany's favor. The French withdrew from the Ruhr and the Germans managed to

Paper money became worthless as the mark's value dropped during the German inflation crisis in 1923. Above: German men and women wait in line for food for their hungry families.

stabilize their currency. The idea that Germany could not be bound by Versailles was already evident.

The uneasy peace

In 1919 the intention had been to prevent a repetition of the recent war by solving those problems which were blamed for its occurrence – a strong militaristic Germany and the demands for national self-determination from ethnic minorities, particularly in the Balkans. Within a year, attempts had been made to introduce appropriate solutions: Germany had been reduced in size, denied strong armed forces, stripped of her colonies and partially surrounded by newly-created "buffer" states; the ethnic minorities of Eastern Europe and the Balkans had been given national identity.

But the solving of one set of problems merely produced another. In Germany, resentment ran high and in many of the new states ethnic minorities still existed. The peace settlement had been rooted in high ideals; in practice its flaws became quickly apparent.

A German Communist poster (left), Nazi poster (above).

CHAPTER 2
THE PRESSURES OF PEACE

In the 1920s, the old society and traditional forms of government were under threat. Nationalism had stirred the peoples of the old imperial powers of Europe and left-wing beliefs were spreading throughout the European working classes. Britain was to have its first socialist government and the same prospect was not far off for France. The Soviet Union was the first country to have a communist government. Yet the Soviet Union shared something important with the European nations being taken over by new right-wing ideologies: it was ruled by a dictator. At times of national crisis, democratic methods seemed too slow and indecisive and the more brutal approach of Fascist or Nazi leaders appeared more likely to succeed. The list of countries falling to dictators of left or right grew worryingly long. Throughout Europe, both right and left made extensive use of propoganda.

The idealism which characterized the actions of the "Big Three" Allied powers at Versailles was based on their unshakable belief in the attractions of democracy. When they set to work breaking up the undemocratic empires of their enemies, they imagined that the new nation states would favor the democratic system. This would, they believed, help to form a community of free nations in Europe.

For a few years after the First World War, this did not seem a completely foolish idea. Poland, Czechoslovakia and Yugoslavia, as well as the defeated nations of Germany and Austria, all opted for democratic government and actively fought against reactionary or revolutionary pressures.

The driving force behind these revolutionary pressures was Russia, Communist since 1917. At first, the problem could be contained. Communist-inspired revolts, particularly in Germany and Austria–Hungary, were put down by elements of the old order before the peace settlement had been finalized. But once the Bolsheviks began to consolidate their power in Russia in 1919, their intention to "export" their new political beliefs through a specially formed Communist International (Comintern), made it clear to the democracies that they were threatened.

Fears of Communist revolution

Despite the creation of Russian-style Communist parties in a number of states in the early 1920s, the revolution proved difficult to spread abroad. The Western Powers had been sufficiently alarmed at the notion of growing Communism to commit forces to oppose the Reds in the Civil War and were to continue to view Russia with a mixture of fear and mistrust. Quite clearly a threat existed, if only in the minds of the Western leaders.

In one sense, this was an unnecessary worry immediately after the Russian Civil War, for Lenin was far more concerned about internal than external policies. He desperately needed to consolidate his power, and for this reason was prepared to delay imposing Communist policies. He allowed a certain amount of private trading and enterprise within his New Economic Policy (NEP), introduced in March 1921. The main purpose of this was to respond to a disastrous famine that had first gripped European Russia in 1920. By the summer of the following year, an estimated 20 to 30 million people had been affected and disease was rife. Lenin's solution was to allow peasants to sell their surplus crops rather than hand them over to the state.

He was vehemently opposed by Trotsky, founder of the Red Army and Commissar for War, who favored stronger central control, industrial growth and international revolution. When Lenin died in January 1924, splits were apparent in the leadership and Russia was in rapid economic decline. The circumstances were ideal for the emergence of a strong leader. Although it was widely expected that this would be Trotsky, he had an underestimated rival in the secretive and ruthless General Secretary of the Communist Party, Joseph Stalin.

Stalin's rise to power

Over the next four years Stalin plotted and schemed his way to supreme power. A gruesome, complicated process of political infighting saw him destroy fellow members of the Politburo – the central governing body – one after another. His chief enemy, Trotsky, may have been intellectually brilliant, but he had no grasp of the realities of political power. As a result, he failed to use his control of the Red Army as a trump card in the struggle and was outmaneuvered by Stalin, who had him exiled in 1929 and murdered in 1940.

Under Stalin, the direction of Communist policy was decisively changed. The policy of world revolution was abandoned in favor of "socialism in one country." Stalin estimated that the Soviet Union was 50 to 100 years behind the more advanced countries in economic development and directed that a supreme effort should be made to close this gap within ten years. He believed that the anti-Communist countries would eventually join together to attack Russia, in order to destroy the revolution. Russia's best defense was to be economically and militarily powerful enough to take on all comers. In pursuit of this objective, he was prepared to commit any brutality and subject his people to a degree of suffering that was to cost millions of lives.

Joseph Stalin in 1920. He dominated the Soviet Union from 1929 until his death in 1953.

Collectivization of agriculture

The first stage of Russia's ordeal was the forced collectivization of the nation's farmland. Collectivization was supposed to create larger units which would produce more grain using less labor by employing modern machinery and methods. After the revolution, the great landowners' estates had been broken up among the peasants and the NEP had seemed to confirm the peasantry as the private owners of the land. By 1928, there were 25 million small holdings averaging 81 hectares (200 acres) in size. The NEP had resulted in the growth of a large *kulak* class of wealthier peasant farmers, who were widely accused of hoarding grain to drive up the price.

In 1928 Stalin decided to confiscate the peasants' land, which would be held and worked collectively, and to liquidate the *kulaks*. Within 10 years, some 98 per cent of Russian farmland had been collectivized and the *kulaks* had been destroyed. Their fate is uncertain, but it is probable that most of them (perhaps 4.5 million) were deported to forced labor camps. It has been estimated that some 3 million *kulaks* died while being deported.

During the process of collectivization the state set very high grain procurement demands to feed the workers in the towns and earn foreign currency through export. If the demands were not met, all grain supplies were confiscated. When there was a poor harvest – as there was in the Ukraine in 1932-33 – a man-made famine resulted which was to cost another 3 million lives.

Russia's industrialization program

These sacrifices were made in order to pay for the industrialization of Russia in two "Five-Year Plans." The first began in 1928 and some impossible targets were set: production of coal was to rise from 39 million tons to at least 75 million tons; steel was to rise from 4.4 million tons to 9 million tons. Few of these targets were met, but impressive progress was made, although at great human cost.

The industrial labor force of 3 million people was doubled and had to endure dreadful housing and inadequate provision for its needs. When production targets were not met, scapegoats were found and hundreds of thousands of innocent people were herded off to forced labor camps, where many died. For example, some 100,000 prisoners died building a canal from the White Sea to the Baltic. By 1934 there were signs of reaction against this merciless pressure.

The Purges

The 17th Congress of the Communist Party met in that year and it seems probable that there was some move to curb Stalin's power. On December 1 Sergei Kirov, Secretary of the Leningrad Party organization, who was considered a potential rival to Stalin, was assassinated. Popular rumor credited Stalin with ordering the killing. If this was true, then Stalin had removed a danger to himself and also proved that a danger to Party leaders existed. This meant emergency measures could be called upon. Stalin unleashed his secret police in a "Great Terror." A purge of enemies, rivals, intellectuals or indeed anyone who showed traces of individualism was begun, and that meant a wave of executions or sentences to slave labor.

No one was safe, although it was better to be an ordinary worker than to be in senior Party circles close to Stalin. When Lenin died, Stalin had been a member of a Politburo of seven. Of the other six, only one escaped Stalin's executioners and that was because he committed suicide before they came for him. At the 17th Congress there were 139 members of the Party's Central Committee and 98 of them were shot. Of 1,966 delegates to the Congress 1,108 perished. Even the secret police themselves were not safe.

The Great Terror effectively ended any spark of opposition to Stalin's rule. People faced torture and death for the slightest sign of independent thought – even for not applauding warmly enough when Stalin's name was mentioned at a local Party meeting. At the cost of millions of lives, Stalin managed to drag Russia from its status as a weak and backward state to one which had great potential strength.

The cost was undoubtedly too high, however, not just in human terms but also in terms of the future security of the state. By 1938, for example, the Red Army had been virtually destroyed by purges that affected up to 20,000 of its officers, many of proven skill. Three of the five pre-purge marshals had died – including Mikhail Tukhachevski, one of the army's youngest and most brilliant commanders, trapped by forged letters provided by the German secret service – and up to 90 per cent of the generals and 80 per cent of the colonels had been imprisoned or shot. The result was a very young and inexperienced officer class. Stalin was to reap the consequences in 1941, when invading German troops defeated his "new" army with ease.

At first the fat capitalist dismisses the Five-Year Plan as "fantasy." Later on he turns green with envy, according to this Soviet propaganda poster.

Combine harvesters in use on a Soviet collective farm

The growth of Italian fascism

A belief in a totalitarian system was not confined to Communists. There were also right-wing movements which gloried in the use of violence. They claimed that dictatorship was superior to democracy, because a dictator was able to make harsh decisions and execute them with a speed and brutality impossible in a free country. One of the first to demonstrate this was the Italian Fascist leader, Benito Mussolini.

Italy had joined the Allies during the First World War in the hope of making territorial gains from the Austro-Hungarian and Turkish empires. These hopes had been largely frustrated by the peace settlement and gave rise to a feeling that the sacrifice of the war had been in vain. Parliamentary democracy in Italy was not working well and the political parties were weak.

By the end of the war there was widespread fear of revolution: the example of Russia's Communist revolution encouraged the left wing and frightened the right. During 1919 and 1920, disorder spread through parts of Italy, with workers going on strike, peasants appropriating the land of large landowners and huge numbers of demobilized soldiers contributing to unrest. This caused many anti-Communists to turn to extreme right-wing groups. By 1921 the most extreme of them were the *Fasci di Combattimento*, combat groups, led by an ex-journalist called Mussolini.

The Fascists, as they were known, had first appeared in 1919, taking their name from the *fasces*, or bundles of reeds used by the Romans as a symbol of authority. At first they advocated setting up a republic, a wealth tax and workers' involvement in managing industry. They organized armed bands, the "Black Shirts," to quell resistance, but it soon became obvious that their violence, coupled with their strong nationalistic and authoritarian aims, alienated many workers. By 1921 Mussolini had changed his plans to attract landowners' and industrialists' support.

This change increased the Fascists' political strength and credibility. They started to make gains, first in local elections and then in national politics. In May 1921 they won 35 seats in the Italian parliament. By 1922 they were strong enough to help counter an attempted general strike, winning popular support by taking over vital public services.

Italy had seemed on the verge of chaos and had been "saved" by the Fascists. Their popularity was high, their opponents were discredited and the Black Shirts were strong, using violence to intimidate anyone who questioned their views. In the first four and a half months of 1921, the Black Shirts killed 207 of their opponents and injured at least 800 more.

Mussolini's march on Rome

The time seemed ripe to seek power, so at the Fascist Convention in Naples in 1922, a motion was put forward to march on Rome, demanding political office. Mussolini's superb oratory – a characteristic of so many of the extremist leaders of the 1920s and 1930s – ensured that the motion was passed on October 24. The march took place four days later. Mussolini traveled by train, arriving in Rome to lead an estimated 25,000 of his followers into the city. The king, Victor Emmanuel III, gave in – perhaps unnecessarily, as alternative political parties did exist – and invited Mussolini to form a government. It was the beginning of a 21-year rule.

Mussolini quickly assumed dictatorial powers. Political opponents were murdered or driven into exile, political parties and trade unions were suppressed, the press was censored and a secret police was set up. By a law passed in 1928, the constitution was changed so that parliament was appointed rather than elected and Mussolini was made Head of Government, appointed by a Fascist Grand Council. This represented the party and state and consisted of Mussolini's chosen lieutenants. Mussolini's grip on power was secure.

Benito Mussolini at a military parade in 1927

Hitler's early political career

Mussolini's sudden rise to dictatorship was an inspiration to ex-corporal Adolf Hitler, who had similar hopes for himself in his adopted Germany (he was Austrian by birth). Germany under the Weimar Republic was a democracy, with such a weak central government that some of its larger states were virtually independent. Hitler launched his political career in and around Munich, the capital of the extremely conservative state of Bavaria. The many anti-Communist local political organizations were tolerated in Bavaria and the violent activities of Hitler's National Socialist (Nazi) Party went unpunished.

Much as he admired Mussolini's successful tactics, Hitler was in no position to seize power. Even locally the Nazis were not absolutely dominant and the party hardly existed outside Bavaria. Unfortunately for Hitler, his first opportunity to overthrow the Bavarian government occurred before his political movement had gathered sufficient strength. In January 1923 the French occupied the Ruhr, causing a political crisis which coincided with a time of massive inflation.

The Beer Hall Putsch

Hitler tried to exploit the mounting unrest. On November 8, 1923 he and his armed followers – known as storm troopers – attended a public rally in a Munich beer hall, where Hitler proclaimed a Nazi revolution. The next day Hitler led a demonstration to overthrow the Bavarian state government, but a volley of shots from a police cordon killed or dispersed his followers and he was arrested. This minor incident came to be known as the "Beer Hall Putsch," and the Nazi propaganda machine later built it up into a major milestone in the nation's life, with the dead storm troopers revered as martyrs.

At the time it seemed that Hitler's political career was finished, but he managed to catch public attention at his trial. He refused to back down and agreed with the prosecution that he had tried to overthrow the state and was proud of it. His lenient judges sentenced him to five years' imprisonment, of which he actually served only nine months.

Hitler's ideas

While in prison Hitler set out his philosophy in a rambling and barely coherent treatise, *Mein Kampf* ("My Struggle"). Hitler believed in the racial superiority of the Aryan people, which included all Germans and many other northern Europeans.

All other races were inferior. Indeed the Slavs (which included the people of Russia and eastern Europe) were subhumans, who should be conquered and exploited by the Aryans. Blacks were even lower than Slavs. However, the Jews were singled out as the main enemy of the Aryans because Hitler considered that they were involved in a conspiracy to control the world.

In *Mein Kampf*, Hitler introduced the idea of German expansion eastward, at the expense of the Slavs. He said Germany needed more "living space for our people." He also denounced all the leading political parties, saying they were in the hands of the Jews. At first the book did not find a market, but eventually it became a best-seller.

Mussolini addresses his loyal Black Shirts in the Forum in Rome, 1934. The Italian Fascists used many of the emblems of Imperial Rome.

The Weimar government's instability

Nazi doctrine only appealed to the masses in desperate times and Germany recovered quickly from the great inflation during 1924. It embarked on a few years of calm and mild prosperity under the leadership of Gustav Stresemann (1923-29). During this time, the Nazi movement grew only slightly. By 1928 there were only 12 Nazi deputies in the *Reichstag* (parliament) out of a total of 608 seats. However, German stability was threatened in 1929 when the world economy slid into recession and Stresemann died.

With the advent of hard times and mass unemployment, many unpopular policies had to be adopted by the ruling coalition of political parties. In March 1930 the Social Democrats, the largest party with 153 seats, left the coalition in protest against proposed cuts in unemployment benefits. In the months that followed, the government tried to govern by Presidential Decree. This meant that the President of Germany, Field Marshal Paul von Hindenburg, who had been elected in 1925, signed decrees and made them law even though the government could not command a majority in the *Reichstag*. This was the first step away from democratic government.

Hitler's growing success

During these months of minority government, there was widespread dissatisfaction and the German people veered to the extremes of left and right. The murderous street fights between the communists and the Nazi storm troopers seemed to add to the popularity of both parties, rather than detract from it. When elections were held in September 1930, the communists had slightly increased the number of their seats to 77, but the Nazis had made astonishing gains to return 107 deputies (18 per cent of the vote).

The appeal of the Nazis continued to grow. Hitler was a gifted orator, propaganda on radio and in newspapers was brilliantly organized and the storm troopers presented an impressive spectacle of force as they goose stepped in parade hundreds of thousands strong. They won support among the millions of unemployed and the frustrated of a defeated nation. Besides this, the democratic system was not working properly with a series of minority governments. The Nazis blamed the Jews and Communists for every failure and promised to make Germany rich and strong again, with government by a strong and decisive leader – Adolf Hitler.

SA (Sturm Abteilungen) *storm troopers demonstrate their strength at a rally in October 1931.*

SA units round up Communist opponents in March 1933.

It was a promise that appealed particularly to businessmen and industrialists – those with most to lose from a socialist revolution – and during the early 1930s Hitler gradually gained their financial and political support. As money flowed from people such as Fritz Thyssen, chairman of United Steelworks, and Hjalmar Schacht, ex-president of the *Reichsbank*, the Nazis stood poised to take over political power. After more squabbling another coalition broke down and further elections were called in July 1932.

Hitler becomes Chancellor

The July 1932 elections resulted in the Nazis becoming the largest party in the *Reichstag*, with 230 deputies returned. However, they did not have an overall majority and Hitler was not called upon to join the government, principally because von Hindenburg had a personal distaste for Hitler. But no coalition could be formed without the Nazis, so more elections were called in November.

The Nazis won only 196 seats, but on January 30, 1933 Hindenburg was finally persuaded to make Hitler Chancellor. He tried to control him by packing the cabinet with conservatives. Hitler simply used his new position to appoint Nazis to crucial posts (an important example was Hermann Goering who was given control of the Prussian police – and Prussia was the largest German state) before demanding new elections in February 1933. During the election campaign the Nazis had a free hand – killing 51 and injuring hundreds of political opponents. On March 5 they had won 288 seats, almost 44 per cent of the vote – but still not an overall majority.

The time had come to seize power. On February 27 the *Reichstag* had been burned down. A Dutch Communist was charged with the crime, but it was almost certainly the work of the Nazis. It enabled Hitler to claim that this was the start of a Communist revolution, and he had most of the Communist deputies and a few social democrat deputies arrested when the newly elected parliament met. This gave him the necessary two-thirds majority to pass an Enabling Act that gave him power to rule without parliament.

In the months that followed, political parties were banned, trade unions were dissolved and education was Nazified. Opponents were thrown into concentration camps and, when von Hindenburg died in August 1934, Hitler completed his power bid by assuming the presidency to go with his chancellorship. This was endorsed by the German electorate in a plebiscite. Hitler now enjoyed total power.

Hitler and President von Hindenburg in 1933

The American postwar boom

One of the conditions which helped Hitler's rise to power was the mass unemployment resulting from the world economic recession, known as the Depression. This crisis began in the United States, which had been enjoying a remarkable boom since the end of the First World War. This prosperity was based on the increased manufacture of durable consumer goods such as radios, automobiles, refrigerators and watches, which benefited from new techniques of mass manufacture.

Under the first two Republican presidents who succeeded President Wilson – Warren Harding and Calvin Coolidge – production and consumption grew impressively: in 1920, 9,000,000 Americans owned automobiles and there were 60,000 radios in American homes; by 1929, Americans owned 26,000,000 automobiles and 10,000,000 radios.

To some extent this boom was a global one. Production rose in Canada, Germany and Italy, while the French had remarkable success in expanding their car manufacturing industry. Even Britain, which was racked by industrial troubles, managed to pay off the debt accumulated during the war and become a creditor nation again. However it was the United States, as the world's creditor for the First World War, that was the keystone of the world's economy. By 1925, the country had become so powerful that it produced 40 per cent of the world's manufactured goods. It was dominant in oil and coal production as well as agricultural output.

Nevertheless there were growing economic problems. In 1922 the Fordney-McCumber Act raised customs duties on imported goods in order to protect US industry from foreign competition. Naturally enough, other countries adopted measures to keep out American-made goods. Within a few years, markets were drying up and it became difficult to sell the US surplus of manufactured goods. By 1927 some companies were beginning to show losses.

The consequences were to be unusually serious, because over a million Americans had been drawn into speculation on the stock market. The danger of this was that shares could be bought "on margin," which meant that only a small percentage of the purchase price was paid immediately and the rest was owed. If shares went up, they could be sold at a profit before the money owed was called for.

Anxious shareholders in Wall Street following the Crash.

The Stock Market Crash

The "on-margin" system saw shares rise to unrealistic values, before it occurred to anyone that prices would have to fall, causing a panic-stricken sale of shares known as "The Stock Market Crash." On one day alone, October 29, 1929, more than 16 million shares were sold on the New York Stock Exchange. Prices plummeted and a number of investors were ruined, unable to repay the banks which had lent them money to buy on margin.

The banks were already in trouble because poor agricultural performance meant that some farm mortgages had been unpaid. So between 1930 and 1932, some 3,500 banks collapsed, together with innumerable companies. Surviving companies laid off workers and the United States suddenly found itself with 15 million jobless. The banking collapse caused many small farmers to lose their mortgaged land and they could not find employment in the already depressed rural areas.

Indeed, in states such as Oklahoma, where the land had been overused to satisfy wartime demands for food and cotton, the soil was no longer workable, having turned to dust as drought and crop disease spread. Hundreds of families took to the roads, trekking west towards California, graphically described in John Steinbeck's *The Grapes of Wrath*.

World trade collapsed and the crisis spread with great speed. The United States had already stopped lending money abroad before the Crash and Germany was feeling these effects by mid-1929. By 1932 over 6 million Germans were unemployed. The British had 3 million unemployed and a sterling crisis in 1931. Banks collapsed in Austria, Hungary, Czechoslovakia, Poland and Germany. Japan's exports of manufactured goods fell by two-thirds and the value of international trade dropped from $3,000,000,000 a month in 1929 to $1,000,000,000 in 1933. Everywhere the effects were the same: long lines of men desperate for work, soup kitchens for women and children and political unrest.

Roosevelt's New Deal

Dissatisfied with Herbert Hoover as President, the American people elected the Democrat Franklin Delano Roosevelt. He took office in March 1933, dedicated to giving Americans a "New Deal" and to fighting the recession.

His proposed platform included the big government spending that his Republican predecessors had avoided. At first many of his policies seemed to promise much and achieve little; but at least he was doing more than simply waiting for the recession to end. Roosevelt's New Deal enjoyed some success and he was re-elected to the White House in 1936, because he had been able to restore the nation's self-confidence. In spite of his policies, the Depression hung over the United States and there were still 9 million out of work.

Britain's internal problems

Unemployment was a mammoth problem in the other Western Powers, Britain and France, where the Depression produced some new ideas but no successful solutions. Indeed, the political history of both countries throughout the 1920s and early 1930s was remarkably similar, reflecting the pressures raised by the trauma of 1914-18 and the general lack of strong leadership at a time of growing social unrest. In Britain, the First World War and its aftermath increased working-class demand for socialist policies, although this was never strong enough to embrace the extremes of Communism. However, the working population contained groups which were working hard for a radical change in British society.

In January 1924, Ramsay MacDonald's Labor Party formed its first government, and raised people's hopes for change. By November, however, the Conservatives had regained office, dedicated to preserving the *status quo*. This increased demands for change, and in May 1926 miners, railwaymen, printers and construction and transport workers acted together in what was known as the General Strike. Stanley Baldwin's government responded, using the army and middle classes to run vital services. In eight days the strike was broken, but a legacy of bitterness remained.

This bitterness showed itself in a split within British society that made political victory difficult for either of the main parties. By the early 1930s the only way to form a workable government was by coalition, forcing both parties to work together. The situation persisted for more than ten years, preventing effective solutions to the social and economic problems of the time.

French instability

In France, successive governments faced the problems of financial strain and social upheaval which resulted from the First World War. Communists won increasing support and, allied to the socialists who had been politically active even before the war, formed an alternative government. However, it was no more successful than the Labor Party in Britain at gaining power. By the early 1930s, ineffectual governments followed one another with monotonous regularity.

The result was a weakening of the two most important European powers. In a sense, such weakness was understandable – the First World War had destroyed the "flower of a generation," leaving a residue of tired and dispirited men – but there was more to it than that. Before 1914 both Britain and France had drawn much of their strength from their empires, which supplied their industries with cheap raw materials. By 1918 these benefits did not seem enough to countries which had had to finance a world war. Both countries also found the United States was threatening their traditional markets and, perhaps most important of all, ideas of independence were beginning to spread throughout their colonial areas, undermining their imperial rule.

The Irish problem

To the British, such nationalist pressure was not new. Even before the First World War they had experienced such feelings much nearer home. Ireland had been a problem for centuries, producing revolts, insurrections and pressures for independence. Successive governments had responded by using force as well as introducing genuine attempts at reform. But the situation was complicated by the existence of Protestant settlers in the north of the island, intent upon continued union with Britain and violently opposed to any political concessions to the majority Roman Catholics in the south.

Feelings ran high on both sides – in 1914, on the eve of the First World War, armed groups of Protestants were ready to use force against the Third Home Rule Bill, designed to grant limited rights to a parliament in Dublin. At Easter 1916, an attempt was made by predominantly Catholic republicans to seize power. The British put down the rising with considerable force, destroying parts of Dublin and executing the captured leaders. Public opinion in Ireland began to swing in favor of independence, causing the British to respond with increased repression.

By 1918, the nationalist *Sinn Fein* ("We Alone") Party had made significant political advances, winning 73 out of 105 Irish seats in the British parliament. The new members of parliament decided to set up their own assembly – the *Dail Eireann* – in Dublin. When this failed to achieve concessions from the British, the Irish Republican Army (IRA) launched a bitter and successful guerrilla war, attacking British officials, police and soldiers. The British once again responded with force, recruiting special police known as "Black and Tans" from the color of their uniforms. Their methods were ruthless; they even burned Cork city center.

When such actions were publicized, British credibility declined and, already war-weary, the government was only too pleased to accept a truce in July 1921. Ireland was divided, with the 26 counties of the south receiving some independence but still loosely under the rule of London. The six counties of the north remained firmly attached to the rest of Britain. Not all nationalists accepted this arrangement – a civil war broke out as soon as the British withdrew and the government in Dublin took two years to establish its rule.

Liberty Hall in Dublin after the Easter Rising in 1916.

Irish government riflemen fighting rebels in July 1922.

Colonial problems

Similar campaigns for independence developed in various parts of both the French and British empires during the 1920s and 1930s. In Africa and the Far East there was little demand for national self-determination, although opposition to British rule in India was growing and the French were beginning to experience trouble in Indochina by the 1930s. The same could not be said of the Middle East, where the collapse of the Turkish empire had raised Arab hopes of independence in the aftermath of the First World War. But these had been cruelly dashed in 1920 when, as a result of the Versailles peace settlement, most of the areas of the Middle East had been passed on to the British and French as mandates.

Arab resentment erupted in anti-French riots in Syria and the beginning of a guerrilla campaign against the British in Mesopotamia (Iraq). The French responded by setting up the separate, Christian-dominated and pro-Western state of Lebanon on the Mediterranean coast of Greater Syria. The British conducted a policing action in Mesopotamia which included, for the first time, a use of Royal Air Force bombers to control inaccessible mountain areas. Neither was a permanent solution. Indeed, by the early 1930s Mesopotamia had been granted virtual independence as Iraq, and both Lebanon and Syria had been promised the same.

Egypt and Palestine

None of these areas was of vital strategic importance to Britain or France, but the same could not be said of Egypt and Palestine. Both acted as protectors of the Suez Canal, a key link in the trade route to India. Although Britain had occupied Egypt as early as 1882, it had left the government in the hands of local rulers, choosing to manipulate rather than control. This allowed Egypt to become a focus for discontent that grew during the 1920s and 1930s. The British responded by maintaining a significant military garrison.

But at least the Egyptians stopped short of open revolt, such as occurred in the recently acquired mandate of Palestine. There the situation was complicated by the so-called "Balfour Declaration" of November 1917, whereby the British had supported the setting up of a Jewish homeland in the area once the First World War was over. In the 1920s a steady trickle of Jews, mainly from Europe, entered Palestine, and this developed into a flood once Hitler had seized power in Germany in 1933.

The British were caught in a dilemma, trapped by their promise of 1917 yet concerned for the future of the local Arab population, which grew increasingly resentful of the Jews. In the end, no effective policies were introduced – attempts to limit Jewish immigration were strongly resisted by those already in Palestine and the failure of this approach alienated the Arabs, who rose in revolt in 1936. For the next three years British troops were to suffer attacks from both sides.

For much of the peacetime period, therefore, neither Britain nor France was free to devote its energies entirely to the problems of European or international politics. Still reeling from the effects of the First World War, struggling to cope with domestic unrest and beset by colonial problems, they were neither willing nor able to take the necessary lead in world affairs. With the only alternative leader, the United States, remaining aloof, the peace settlement so laboriously established in 1919 stood little chance of surviving.

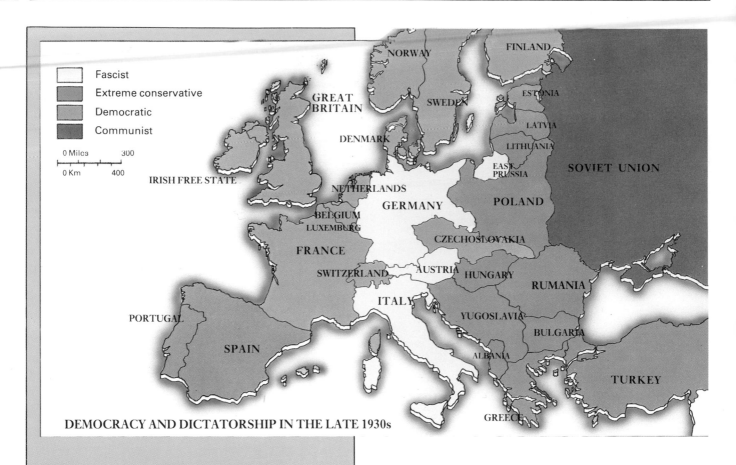

Fascist

Extreme conservative

Democratic

Communist

0 Miles   300

0 Km   400

DEMOCRACY AND DICTATORSHIP IN THE LATE 1930s

CHAPTER 3
THE FAILURE OF THE LEAGUE

The only powers with a real interest in preserving the order established at Versailles after the First World War were Britain and France. The United States was sunk in isolation and offered no help as Britain and France tried to uphold the League of Nations as the champion of peace. Their efforts were threatened by the aggressive regimes of dictators, who were not afraid to use war to achieve their aims of acquiring more territory. Again and again, the League of Nations and the democracies failed to stop the aggression of these opponents, in Italy, Germany and Spain. With each failure, these regimes seemed stronger and more attractive, and democracy weaker.

The delegates at the various peace conferences in 1919 and 1920 had hoped that the creation of the League of Nations would resolve international disputes without war. The League came into being in January 1920 and enjoyed a decade of success. Although these years were not completely free from conflict, there was no obvious failure of the League to prevent conflict. Some of the major wars that occurred – such as the Russo-Polish War of 1920 – were simply not referred to the League. Other events, such as the Irish struggle for independence, could not be brought before the League. In this case it was because Ireland was then regarded as part of Britain.

Despite these limitations, the League had some achievements to its credit. It resolved a serious dispute between Sweden and Finland over the Aaland Islands in 1920. It also prevented Britain and Turkey going to war over the city of Mosul in 1923-24, when a League Commission made the embarrassing revelation that the inhabitants of Mosul hated the British and the Turks equally. On two other occasions it even managed to halt conflicts: a Greek invasion of Bulgaria in 1925 and a Peruvian attack on Colombia in 1932.

Despite this, there were serious weaknesses in the League's ability to deal with any particularly determined and powerful member state. All the member nations were equal and had just one vote in the League Assembly; but decisions there had to be unanimous and the Assembly could only recommend, not implement, action. It was therefore only a debating chamber and it was in the League's Council that important action had to be initiated.

It was originally intended that the five victorious Allies – the United States, France, Britain, Italy and Japan – would dominate the Council as permanent members able to outvote the four temporary members elected by the Assembly. The US refusal to join the League spoiled this, and although Germany (in 1926) and Russia (in 1934) became permanent members, the Great Powers could always be outvoted by temporary members whose numbers had risen to nine. Another problem was that the Council's decision on important matters had to be unanimous. The fatal drawback, however, was that none of the permanent members had the will or the strength to make the League stand up to an aggressor.

Diplomatic maneuvers

While the general situation remained unstable, there were some isolated instances of improved relations between countries and some arms limitation. For various reasons the three greatest naval powers – Britain, the USA and Japan – were all interested in limiting the size of their navies and preventing an arms race in shipbuilding. The British felt the financial hardship of maintaining a great fleet. The United States was quite satisfied with any arrangement that guaranteed its security. Japan would accept a fleet only two-thirds the size of the Royal Navy and US Navy, because it gave the Japanese local superiority in the Pacific, which was all that mattered to Japanese admirals.

These attitudes resulted in the apparent success of the Washington Naval Conference of 1921-22, which tried to limit the size of the world's main navies. Some reductions were negotiated in terms of capital ships (battleships and battle cruisers), but by 1935, when Britain agreed to a larger German Navy in the Anglo-German Naval Pact, most powers were building up their aircraft carriers, destroyers and frigates.

There was also superficial success in fostering treaties between member states. In the Locarno treaties of 1925, Britain and Italy agreed to act as guarantors of the frontiers in Western Europe and agreed to intervene if there was any "flagrant" violation of the provisions of Versailles. It was the use of the word "flagrant" that later enabled both states to ignore their obligations to security in Western Europe.

In the long run, therefore, the Locarno treaties proved worthless and they were succeeded by an even more pointless diplomatic exercise – the Kellogg-Briand Pact of 1928. More than 60 nations signed this Pact to "outlaw war," but it had no obvious effect upon any of them. It stands as a sad but fitting monument to the League – the constant expression of good intentions without the power to enforce them.

A 1938 meeting of the League of Nations

Japan and China

This shortcoming was demonstrated when Japan left the League in 1933. The Japanese had always been somewhat unlikely permanent Council members of an organization dedicated to peace, when their obvious ambition was supremacy in the Far East. Their first target was the conquest of China. The Chinese were initially a helpless prey and quite unable to resist the concessions to Japan made at the postwar peace conference (temporary occupation of Tsingtao and Shantung). This was because most of China was fragmented and ruled by warlords.

The only Chinese organizations with any intention of uniting and reforming China were the Kuomintang (a socialist, democratic and nationalist party founded in 1912) and the Chinese Communist Party (founded in 1921). For a while the Kuomintang and the Communists were firm allies, both enjoying military support from the Soviet Union, but they disagreed in 1926, shortly after Chiang Kai-shek became the undisputed leader of the Kuomintang.

Civil war broke out in April 1927 when Chiang ordered his men to turn on the Communists. At first the Kuomintang was highly successful, gaining control

Japanese troops enter a village near Hsuchow.

CHINA 1927–1935

→ Route of the Long March
October 1934–October 1935

■ Communist-held areas 1927–34

Japanese occupied areas 1935

0 Miles 400
0 Km 600

SOVIET UNION

MANCHURIA

MONGOLIA

MUKDEN

Huang Ho

CHINA

PEKING

KOREA

TSINGTAO

SHANTUNG

YENAN

SHENSI

HSUCHOW

NANKING

SHANGHAI

Yangtze

SZECHUAN

HUNAN

KIANGSI

TAIWAN

CANTON

HONG KONG

FRENCH INDOCHINA

of most of China and defeating the Communists, who regrouped under the leadership of Mao Tse-tung in Kiangsi and Hunan provinces. The Communists remained in the Kiangsi-Hunan provinces until 1934, when Kuomintang pressure intensified and they embarked on an 11,600-km (7,200-mile) retreat known as the "Long March" to the remote Yenan province in the northwest.

By the end of 1936 there was another shaky alliance between the Communists and the Kuomintang to try to preserve Chinese unity in the face of the Japanese threat. However, mutual suspicion persisted.

Japan invades China

As far as the Japanese were concerned, Chinese unity threatened their plans for supremacy in the Far East. The key to their plans was the domination of Manchuria, China's most industrialized province, in which they had trade interests. The Japanese government hoped to do this either by setting up a puppet government there or by genuine cooperation with the Chinese. The generals commanding the Japanese Army preferred outright conquest and faked a sabotage incident on the Mukden railway on September 18, 1931. The Chinese were blamed for this and the Japanese Army promptly occupied the whole of Manchuria. Belatedly and timidly, the League decided to deal with this act of aggression.

The only two powers able to intervene militarily in the Far East were the United States and the Soviet Union, neither of which belonged to the League. Realizing its weakness, the League of Nations Commission on the affair put forward a very weak condemnation of Japan in 1933. It condemned Japan for using force but added that Japan's grievances about the situation in Manchuria were justified. No action was to be taken against the Japanese, who, nevertheless, withdrew from the League in protest.

Mussolini defies the League

One of the reasons for this was that the League was giving up hope of preserving peace in the face of determined aggression. After Japan, the next power to put the League to the test was Italy, another permanent Council member. The Italian dictator Mussolini was determined upon colonial expansion to win military glory for his regime. In a long, drawn-out drama he forced a quarrel upon Ethiopia because of border disputes and incidents between Ethiopian forces and the garrison of Italian Somaliland in December 1934.

On the face of it, Mussolini was taking a far greater risk in breaking the League Charter because one of the League's most powerful members, Britain, was capable of devastating intervention. Italy is a vulnerable peninsula and the Royal Navy was four times as powerful as the Italian fleet. Besides this, the British garrison in Egypt dominated the Suez Canal, which could cut Somaliland off from Italy. But Mussolini gambled on the fact that the British had no real interest in protecting Ethiopia, preferring to maintain friendship with Italy. Indeed, both Britain and France were eagerly cultivating an Italian alliance against the resurgent Germany of Adolf Hitler.

The Italian preparations for war were lengthy and obvious as they built up their forces in East Africa to 250,000 men. It was apparent that Britain and France were reluctant to oppose Mussolini, so supporters of the League in Britain organized an unofficial "Peace Ballot" in late 1934. The surprising result was that some 10 million voters favored economic sanctions against an aggressor and 6 million agreed to the use of military force against aggression. The British government was caught between a desire for Italian friendship and a need to placate an electorate which was in favor of firm, even violent, measures to restrain Italy.

The Italian invasion of Ethiopia

Mussolini kept his nerve even though the British Home Fleet sailed for the Mediterranean in September. On October 3, 1935 the Italian forces in East Africa moved across the frontiers of Eritrea and Italian Somaliland into Ethiopia. They had tanks, mustard gas and an air force to back them, while their Ethiopian opponents were short of fire-arms and carried swords and spears.

At first the Italians brushed off Ethiopian attackers fairly easily, but made painfully slow progress over the roadless and sparsely populated terrain. A League Committee recommended that sanctions be adopted against Italy as punishment for aggression. The League Assembly voted to impose economic sanctions, although in private the French Foreign Minister assured Italy that its oil supplies would be kept up. At no point was military action contemplated, despite the fact that Ethiopia was a member of the League.

While the League failed to take effective action, the Italian armies in Ethiopia were given a new, more vigorous commander, General Pietro Badoglio. The Italians used their artillery and air power with some skill to cover their advance, inflicting heavy casualties on their enemy.

Victory in Ethiopia

By mid-March only the Emperor, Haile Selassie, remained in the field with an undefeated army. Haile Selassie was no soldier but, determined to do his duty and fight, on March 31 he led an ill-armed force of 30,000 men against prepared Italian positions at Mai Ceu. The Ethiopians were beaten off with losses of 10,000 men and their retreat became a rout.

Only the remnants of his Imperial Guard saved the Emperor, who reached his capital, Addis Ababa, at the end of April. He failed to rally further support and went into exile in Britain, leaving the Italians to enter Addis Ababa in triumph on May 5. The fighting was over and all that remained was for the Italians to pacify their conquest, with Badoglio named as viceroy.

The Ethiopian campaign was another milestone on the road to general war. Before his campaign had brought League sanctions down on him, Mussolini had not been an admirer of Hitler. Indeed, Italian interests in Austrian border territory had placed him squarely on the side of Britain and France in restraining German ambitions. But the ineffective display of opposition from Britain and France made him turn to Germany as the most likely potential ally.

It was not only that Italian and German interests were compatible but also that Mussolini and Hitler were both dictators, ruling states where they faced no opposition because only one party was allowed. Fascists and Nazis were equally devoted to military solutions to problems, as well as being anti-democratic and anti-Communist. They were soon ranged on the same side in a major international crisis that finally destroyed the League's effectiveness – the Spanish Civil War.

The origins of the Spanish Civil War

It is a tragic truth that Spanish society in the 1930s was so divided that a war was virtually inevitable. By 1931, the centuries-old monarchy was so widely unpopular that the king, Alfonso XIII, fled, allowing Spain to become a republic and a democracy. The first elected government was liberal and failed to make sweeping reforms. Church burning and the murder of priests and landowners' agents had become a common form of protest. The public reaction against this led to the election of a right-wing government in 1933.

The left responded to the new government with a call for a general strike and, in October 1934, there was an armed uprising in Asturias. The government turned to the only troops it could rely on, the Spanish Foreign Legion and the *regulares*, North African mercenaries recruited from Spanish Morocco. These professional soldiers put down the uprising with great ferocity, killing or wounding 2,000 rebels.

This did not put an end to the political unrest. In February 1936, a Popular Front of Radicals, Socialists and Communists was elected. By June, plans for a military coup by the right wing were well advanced. In July, General Francisco Franco was smuggled into Spanish Morocco, where he rallied the Army of North Africa and invaded mainland Spain.

The Italians advance into Ethiopia slowly because of the poor roads and rough terrain.

Spain divided

The Nationalists (as Franco's rebels called themselves) had started the war with a ready-made army and they made swift progress, dealing with resistance in areas sympathetic to their cause. The Republicans (the government side) did not have the armed forces on their side, but they had popular support.

By the end of July 1936, the Nationalists had established themselves in northern and western Spain with the exception of Asturias, the Basque Provinces and Catalonia. The rest was Republican territory but, of course, there were millions of right-wingers in Republican areas and Communists in Nationalist areas. This provoked massacres and atrocities. About 100,000 perished in July and August as victims of personal or class revenge. Some 500,000 people are estimated to have died during the war as a result of lynchings or executions behind the front line.

Once they had consolidated their position, the Nationalists decided to advance on the capital, Madrid. But fears that his forces were not strong enough to take Madrid persuaded Franco to make for Toledo, which was under siege by Republican forces. Toledo was secured at the end of September. By November his tired army had reached Madrid, temporarily abandoned by the Republican government. Republican forces however, led a counterattack which regained Madrid. It was to remain a Republican bastion until the end of the war.

Foreign aid

During the three years that the war lasted (1936-39), the Nationalists received help from the Nazis and Fascists on a major scale. In the very beginning, Franco's Army of North Africa was ferried to the mainland by German and Italian aircraft. Some 10,000 Germans served in the "volunteer" Condor Legion – the best armed troops on either side, with powerful tank, anti-tank and aircraft units. Mussolini sent more than 50,000 troops, grouped in several divisions, supporting them with large naval and air forces based in Majorca. Portugal was also a dictatorship, under President Antonio Salazar, and a Portuguese Legion of 20,000 men eventually joined the fight for the Nationalists.

More important perhaps than the men were the modern weapons, which the Fascist countries provided and used for the Nationalist cause. For the Nazis and Fascists, the Spanish conflict was a proving ground for their modern tanks and aircraft.

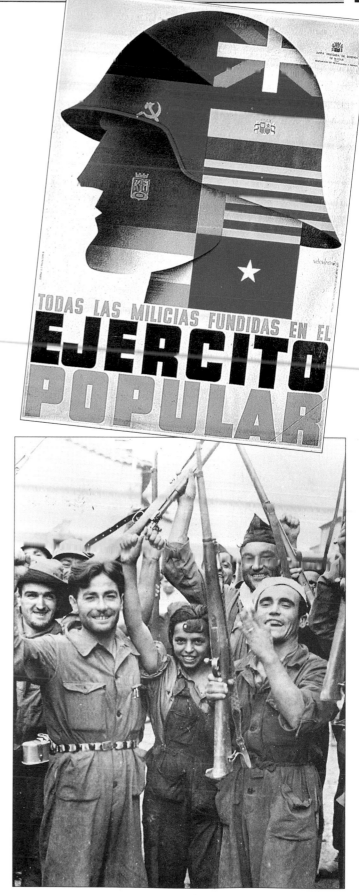

Top: A Republican poster urges all armed groups to join the People's Army.
Above: Recruits for the Republican forces.

This was particularly the case with the German Condor Legion. By 1938, Junkers Ju 87 Stuka dive-bombers had made their appearance, hitting Republican targets and demoralizing their defenders prior to assault by armor and infantry.

The Republicans eventually received support from Communist Russia. Stalin gained a financial advantage when the Republican Finance Minister shipped most of Spain's 760-ton gold reserve, one of the largest in the world, to the Soviet Union as security for supplies of oil and weapons. The Russians provided advisors and pilots for the aircraft they supplied, although the major manpower reinforcement for the Republicans came from the International Brigades.

These included 10,000 French, 5,000 Germans and Austrians, 2,800 Americans and 2,000 British. Some 40,000 men from 50 different countries joined the International Brigades. These men were not particularly well-trained or natural soldiers but they fought hard in every major engagement, until their disbandment in November 1938.

Both sides paused for breath after the Nationalist failure to take Madrid. In February 1937, the Nationalists pressed towards the capital again. This time they were heavily defeated at the bloody Battle of Jarama. After Jarama the Republican International Brigades and Popular Army advanced to Guadalajara, where they routed the Italian Corps. Madrid had been shelled

Madrid was constantly under attack by German bombers.

and bombed for four months, but Jarama and Guadalajara reflected a turn in the tide. Newly supplied Soviet tanks and planes gave the Republicans a chance of fighting on equal terms.

The Nyon Conference

At no point did the League of Nations interfere. Mussolini's Ethiopian adventure had exposed its weakness and it became irrelevant as a force in international relations. However, the Spanish conflict could not be ignored, because of the intervention of Italy, Germany and the Soviet Union. The Western Powers invited those countries to meet at Nyon in Switzerland, in September 1937, to discuss the issue.

The British favored a policy of non-intervention and although France, Germany, Italy and Russia outwardly agreed with this, in fact they actually ignored it. The only effective result came from a British threat to sink all unidentified submarines in the western Mediterranean. The Italians had been using submarines to sink cargo vessels supplying the Republicans, but this activity ceased abruptly after Nyon.

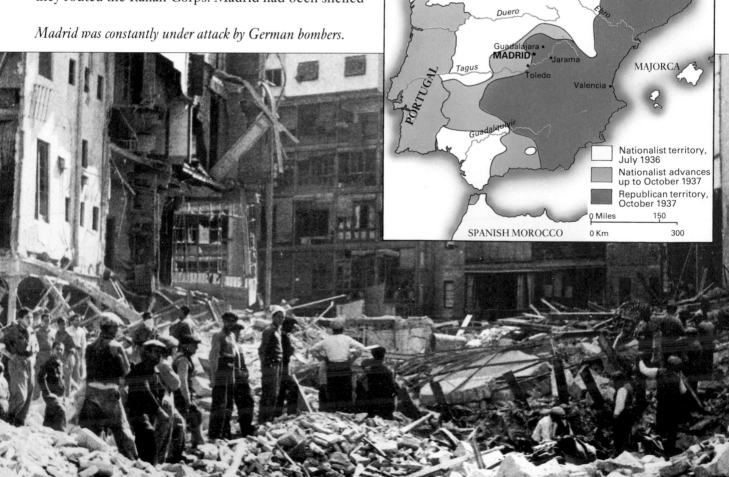

THE SPANISH CIVIL WAR, JULY 1936-OCTOBER 1937

Nationalist territory, July 1936

Nationalist advances up to October 1937

Republican territory, October 1937

The Nationalists take northern Spain

The Republican enclaves of Asturias and the Basque country did not have Soviet aircraft and tanks to defend them. They were at the mercy of the bombers of the Condor Legion, which razed the market towns of Durango and Guernica. Foreign reaction to these atrocities was so strong that the Nationalists tried to deny that they were to blame and then claimed that the bombing had been a mistake. The important thing from their point of view, however, was the success of their tactics, which resulted in the capture of Bilbao and the ending of all resistance in northern Spain outside Catalonia by October 1937.

Although northern Spain was doomed, the Republicans carried out three major offensives to try to halt the Nationalist advance on Catalonia, Aragon and New Castile. But the Nationalists, with new German Messerschmitt and Heinkel aircraft and improved Italian Savoias, drove the Soviet aircraft from the skies. Nationalist artillery was also superior and their equipment was in better supply.

At first the Republicans succeeded at Brunete, but then they were driven back with heavy losses. It was the same story at Belchite in northern Aragon later in August. An attack on Teruel in southern Aragon in December repeated the pattern of early Republican success, followed by disaster as the Nationalists counterattacked in January and February 1938.

Republican supporters flee to France in 1939.

The Nationalist victory

By the summer of 1938, the Republicans seemed to be engaged in a hopeless struggle. The Republican commanders decided on a last great offensive, in July 1938, across the River Ebro to try to stave off defeat. After five months' fighting, the Republicans were exhausted and the Nationalists slowly pushed forward against ever decreasing resistance.

In January 1939, Barcelona fell and 400,000 refugees from Nationalist vengeance fled across the French border. By the end of March, Madrid had fallen and on April 1 Franco announced that the war was over. In the process of eradicating opposition, over 150,000 Republicans were executed over the next four years. It is estimated that some 802,000 people died as a result of the Spanish Civil War.

While the Spanish had been fighting their civil war, the relations between the Western Powers and Germany had deteriorated. The League of Nations was no longer a force in international disputes and the European nations were gradually drawing closer and closer to world war.

OCTOBER 1937–FEBRUARY 1939

Guernica · FRANCE
Bilbao · Durango
Ebro
CATALONIA
Duero
ARAGON
Belchite · Barcelona
Brunete · MADRID · Teruel
Tagus · Toledo · MAJORCA
NEW CASTILE
PORTUGAL
Guadalquivir

☐ Nationalist territory, October 1937
☐ Nationalist advances up to February 1939
☐ Republican territory, February 1939

SPANISH MOROCCO

0 Miles 150
0 Km 300

Hitler reviews SA formations at a rally in Dortmund, 1933.

CHAPTER 4
THE ROAD TO WORLD WAR

War was inevitable from the moment Hitler came to power in Germany. For a long time the European democracies refused to believe this and unsuccessfully tried to appease German ambitions. Their efforts to avoid war meant that they initially gave in to Hitler's demands. Hitler began as the dictator of an unarmed and isolated country, which he made into a powerful military force, allied both to Italy and Japan. The French and British were slow to recognize the danger. After the German occupation of Czechoslovakia, they finally realized that they would have to make a stand against Hitler. But in the last months before the clash of arms, they failed to win over the Soviet Union as an ally against the right-wing dictatorships that opposed them. Hitler invaded Poland and thus started the Second World War. Knowing that he would only have to fight against Britain and France, he was confident that his army could take them on.

Nothing had greater significance in Europe's slide towards general war than Hitler's personality and the nature of his regime. Those who voted for and enabled Hitler to seize power were expressing German nationalism. They were frustrated by the continuing status of Germany as a defeated power and angry at the Weimar Government's social and economic failure, which resulted in 6 million unemployed in 1932. In voting for Hitler they had voted for more than a nationalist leader who would right their wrongs; they had voted for a man who told them that they were the elite race.

Perhaps few Germans realized the limitless nature of Nazi ambitions when Hitler first came to power, although most of them seemed to appreciate the sudden surge of unity and confidence that occurred. After years of weak government and constant elections, the fact that Hitler brutally eradicated any opposition seems to have been reassuring rather than frightening to his people. In a plebiscite held on November 12, 1933, 92 per cent of Germans voted for Nazi candidates (there were no opposition candidates) and 93 per cent of them agreed with his withdrawal from the Geneva Disarmament Conference and the League of Nations.

The Nazi regime

This result was surprising in that, even by November 1933, the intolerant nature of the Nazi regime had been made obvious enough. Hitler seized power on March 23, 1933 and his opponents were immediately under attack. The anti-Nazis in the various state governments were driven from power or thrown into concentration camps.

Trade union leaders were invited to a huge workers' rally on May Day 1933, returning to find their offices occupied by storm troopers who beat them up and herded them off to concentration camps. All German workers became members of a single Nazi union, the German Workers' Front, and trade union activity was banned. Next came the political parties. Their offices were seized and their assets confiscated before the Nazi Party was made the only legal political organization on July 14.

The Nuremberg rallies

Once in power, the Nazis continued to stage-manage impressive parades and events. Every year there was a rally for the party faithful at Nuremberg in September. This consisted of several days of military parades, flashlight processions and speeches by Nazi leaders in a specially constructed amphitheater.

Another event which was staged to impress the outside world with German superiority was the 1936 Olympic Games. Although German athletes won many medals a US black athlete, Jesse Owens, stole the show by winning four gold medals.

The persecution of the Jews

In September 1935 the Nazis made their persecution of the Jews official by passing the Nuremberg Laws. These deprived all Jews of German citizenship, forbade marriage between Germans and Jews and stopped Jews employing German servants.

This was only one part of a long campaign of humiliation and harassment, punctuated by violence and murder, which culminated in the "final solution" – the slaughter of the Jews. It is estimated that up to 6 million Jews died in what is known as "The Holocaust." By the mid-1930s it must have been obvious to most Germans that the Nazi regime was prepared to take the most extreme measures against its opponents.

An anti-Jewish banner in 1935 proclaims "The Jews are our misfortune."

The Night of the Long Knives

With the Nazification of justice and education, only the armed forces could possibly threaten Hitler's hold on power. In the Germany of 1934 there were three separate armed groups. There was the regular army, the *Reichswehr*, limited to 100,000 by the Treaty of Versailles, and there were a few thousand of Hitler's personal and blindly loyal guards, the *Schütz Staffeln* (SS). In addition to them was the much larger and more uncontrollable force of brown-shirted storm troopers, known as the *Sturm Abteilungen* (SA), who numbered between 2 to 3 million and were under the command of one of Hitler's most important and powerful lieutenants, Ernst Roehm. On June 30, 1934 Hitler liquidated Roehm and the SA. This became known as the "Night of the Long Knives."

Using the SS, Hitler ordered the round-up and execution of Roehm and the SA leadership. The official reason for this was the accusation that the SA leadership was plotting against Hitler, but there were also rumors that Hitler was disgusted by their homosexuality. There were 77 names on the list of people to be executed, although another 100 to 300 died in the bloodbath, including some of Hitler's personal enemies. After this stunning blow, the SA were disarmed and downgraded into a sports club.

Hitler surrounded by members of the SA, shortly before the Night of the Long Knives.

German soldiers demonstrate anti-aircraft guns at a rally in 1935.

Hitler and the Army

The Army welcomed the destruction of the SA, which had seemed a dangerous rival military force. However, it was next in line. Hitler was too devoted to the ideal of the German Army at this stage of his career to wish to change it radically, but he did want to be sure that it was utterly under his control – particularly as he planned a vast expansion of the German armed forces in his quest to reverse the concessions made by the Weimar politicians at Versailles.

After the death of von Hindenburg in August 1934, Hitler became President and the armed forces were required to make a personal oath of allegiance to him. Nothing was more important to Hitler than that Germany should have extremely powerful armed forces. This feeling was shared by the German people, who had long resented the fact that the Treaty of Versailles had limited German forces and merely expressed a pious hope that other countries would disarm. They had not disarmed and the French Army was still able to mobilize 90 divisions. It seemed only fair that Germany should abolish this inequality and there was a general desire to begin rearming.

German rearmament

There is some evidence that the Germans had been ignoring the limitations of Versailles on their armed forces even before Hitler came to power. Indeed, as early as the Treaty of Rapallo with Russia in 1922, elements of the *Reichswehr* had trained with the Red Army. They had conducted the first in a series of experiments in the use of tanks (possession of which was banned by Versailles) that was to culminate in the creation of Panzer (tank) divisions and the development of mobile warfare, known as *Blitzkrieg* (lightning war).

At the same time, various aircraft manufacturers, under the guise of producing passenger planes, had begun to develop bombers and fighter machines. Pilots for the latter had been trained under the auspices of Nazi-controlled glider schools or in the commercial airline, *Lufthansa*.

In March 1935, Hitler formally announced his rearmament policy, confident that the Western Powers would not move against him. On March 9, the Allied governments were told something they had long suspected, that the *Luftwaffe* (German Air Force) was already in existence. On March 16 it was announced that the German Army would be increased to 36 divisions, but it is probable that German rearmament did not begin in earnest until spring 1936.

It would have been perfectly legitimate for the Allies to have taken this declaration of rearmament as a violent breach of the Versailles Treaty, and justification for attacking Germany. They undoubtedly still had the strength to do so at the time, but they were hesitant and divided. The French would not move without British support, but the British did not feel the German Army presented such a threat as did the French. The latter had already begun to build defenses, the Maginot Line, along the frontier with Germany.

Besides this, some people in Britain felt that the provisions of Versailles had indeed been unfair, and that a reasonable level of German rearmament could be justified. Hitler was also clever enough to pacify the British, by ruling out a naval arms race with them. In June 1935, the Anglo-German Naval Treaty was signed, limiting Germany to 35 per cent of the strength of Britain's surface fleet.

This Treaty signaled a definite split between the French and the British. It had been made without any consultation between the Allies, despite the fact that it legitimized an increase in the size of the German Navy, which contravened the terms of Versailles. At a time when it was vital for the Western Powers to be sure of one another, the British had given the French cause to distrust them.

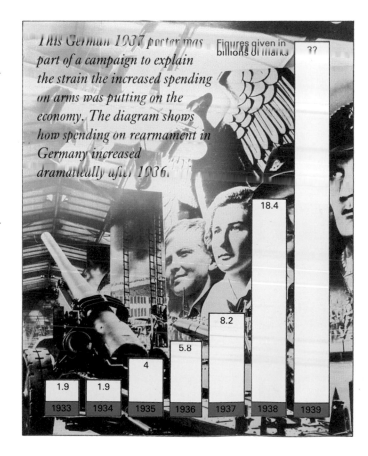

This German 1937 poster was part of a campaign to explain the strain the increased spending on arms was putting on the economy. The diagram shows how spending on rearmament in Germany increased dramatically after 1936.

Figures given in billions of marks

1933	1934	1935	1936	1937	1938	1939
1.9	1.9	4	5.8	8.2	18.4	??

Once German rearmament had begun, it seemed to proceed with terrifying speed. Some of this was an illusion which was deliberately produced by the Nazi propaganda machine. Hitler calculated quite rightly that fear of his power would make the Allies think twice before interfering with his plan to revise the Versailles settlement. A constant series of military parades and displays of the weapons most feared by his potential enemies (tanks and aircraft), succeeded in giving an impression of fearsome strength.

This was particularly the case with the *Luftwaffe*. Its size (erroneously estimated by the British in 1935 as 2,500 front-line aircraft – an exaggeration of perhaps 500 per cent) and especially its preponderance of bombers, was of major concern to Britain and France. With the memory of German air raids on England in 1917-18, in which 1,400 people had died, there was a very real fear that strategic bombing in a future war would have a devastating effect. Indeed, by 1939 the British government was predicting up to 70,000 civilian casualties in the first week of hostilities alone. Also, despite the introduction of radar and the deployment of fast effective fighters like the Spitfire and Hurricane, it showed no confidence that the bombers would be stopped.

The march into the Rhineland

This element of fear worked as Hitler pursued a course of whittling down the restrictions of Versailles. His first step had been withdrawal from the League of Nations in October 1934 and then an open avowal of rearmament when his forces were no match for the French Army. After these successes he became bolder and more provocative. On March 7, 1936 the German Army marched into the Rhineland, the buffer zone between France and Germany, which had been demilitarized at Versailles.

This further and major breach of the Treaty was another gamble. Hitler's generals could only find one division at short notice to perform this operation and only three battalions actually crossed the Rhine. Obviously the French could easily have disposed of this small force and they should have had the backing of Britain and Italy, who were guarantors of the Locarno settlement which confirmed the demilitarization of the Rhineland. Unfortunately all three powers were preoccupied with Italy's attack on Ethiopia at the time, so another German transgression of Versailles went unchallenged. Hitler's confidence in dealing with foreign affairs grew.

The United States opts for isolation

During the 1930s, the United States kept out of European affairs. The world economic crisis and Depression meant the American people wanted their government to concentrate on internal matters. President Roosevelt realized this, but he also understood that the United States could not ignore Hitler and remain in isolation. He tested the atmosphere with a speech about international problems in 1937, but found that isolationism had a very strong hold on the American people. If Roosevelt intervened in European affairs, he risked becoming very unpopular. So the United States remained uninvolved in the growing crisis in Europe.

The Axis

The reoccupation of the Rhineland was succeeded by another propaganda coup: the announcement of the construction of fortifications along Germany's western border, the Siegfried Line. In 1936, Germany also consolidated her position by a system of alliances.

In November 1936, Italy and Germany were allied in the "Rome-Berlin Axis" and then Japan joined Germany in the "Anti-Comintern Pact." The worst nightmares of British and French statesmen seemed to have been realized. Italy, the only significant European power still unaligned, had taken Germany's side. If Germany became involved in a European war, Japan (the world's third largest naval power) would attack Allied possessions in the Far East. From this moment on, Britain and France were not so much concerned with enforcing the conditions of Versailles as they were with preventing war. The French tried to counter the new alliance structure through alliances with the "Little Entente" powers of Czechoslovakia, Yugoslavia and Rumania – but to no real effect.

Italy had a heavy price to pay for a German alliance. The Versailles settlement had forbidden *Anschluss* (the union of Austria and Germany) and, as Italy had shorn off a slice of Austrian territory as her reward for being on the winning side in 1918, it was important to Mussolini that he should not have a powerful state to the north, capable of reclaiming its lost territory.

But as Germany's ally, he could hardly object to *Anschluss* and, after September 1937, he was afraid to. During that month he visited Germany and saw convincing evidence of the scale of German rearmament. Parades of tens of thousands of heavily equipped soldiers, vast army maneuvers, a visit to a huge armament factory and a rally of 800,000 Nazis were created by Hitler to impress the Italian dictator.

The Anschluss

However the Austrian Chancellor, Dr Kurt von Schuschnigg, was not prepared to surrender his country to German domination. In February 1938, he was summoned to meet Hitler, who attacked him for his alleged ill-treatment of Austrian Nazis. Hitler then browbeat him into appointing a Nazi Minister of the Interior – an important office, carrying control over the police. On his return to Austria, Schuschnigg tried to frustrate Hitler's plans by holding a plebiscite on the *Anschluss* question. He was certain that the Austrian people would reject it, but Hitler would not allow him to find out. The Nazi Minister of the Interior obeyed instructions to appeal for German help to avoid internal disorder. Hitler paused only to get Mussolini's agreement and then invaded on March 12. On the next day the union of Austria with Germany was proclaimed.

Once again Britain and France watched helplessly. The only leader who could intervene was Mussolini and he was Hitler's ally. The Western Powers consoled themselves with the argument that *Anschluss* was not an unreasonable German desire – given the fact that the Austrians were a German-speaking people, who massively endorsed union with Germany by a 99.5 per cent vote on April 10, only one month after it had been successfully accomplished.

The 1938 party rally at Nuremberg. These spectacles impressed many foreign visitors, including Mussolini.

Legend:
- Czech territory given to Germany by Munich Agreement, September 1938
- Czech territory occupied by Poland, October 1938
- Czech territory occupied by Hungary, November 1938, March 1939

GERMANY

SUDETENLAND • PRAGUE

BOHEMIA

CZECHOSLOVAKIA

POLAND

GERMANY

TESCHEN

0 Miles 50
0 Km 100

MORAVIA

AUSTRIA

SLOVAKIA

RUTHENIA

SLOVAK TERRITORY

HUNGARY

RUMANIA

THE BREAK-UP OF CZECHOSLOVAKIA

The German "invasion" of Austria had been bloodless. It was also the first major undertaking made by the German armed forces with Hitler as their Commander-in-Chief. The German leader had never been happy about the loyalty or zeal of the military commanders who were in charge when he came to power. They had objected to the haste with which the army was to be expanded, they had not produced an impressive force for his march into the Rhineland and they sealed their fate when they objected to his plans for *Anschluss*. They believed that there was a grave risk of war with France and that Germany was not yet strong enough to win that struggle.

Hitler did not directly control the armed forces. He now moved to change that. The Commander-in-Chief of all three services, army, navy and air force, was Field Marshal Werner von Blomberg. He was trapped into a marriage with an ex-prostitute and forced to resign in January 1938. The Army Commander, General Werner von Fritsch, was framed on very flimsy evidence of homosexuality and resigned "for health reasons" in February. Hitler took over Blomberg's position himself and made the compliant General Walther von Brauchitsch his Army Commander. A clean sweep of possible opposition was then made, with the dismissal of 16 senior generals and the transfer of some 44 others.

The Sudeten problem

After the *Anschluss*, it is all too evident in hindsight that Czechoslovakia was next on Hitler's list. Hitler's Greater German *Reich* (Empire) now surrounded western Czechoslovakia and there was a sizable German minority – some 3,250,000 – in the Sudetenland, which had been incorporated into the Czech state by the Treaty of Versailles. Czechoslovakia was, however, a far harder nut to crack. It had 35 well-equipped divisions and a strong alliance with France. Hitler set his plan in motion. In April 1938, the Sudeten Nazi leader, Konrad Henlein, demanded impossible concessions from the Czech government and German troops were moved up to the border. The Czechs responded by ordering a general mobilization of their army.

The mobilization stiffened the mood of the British and French, who had been urging the Czechs to be conciliatory. They now warned Hitler that he risked a general war over Czechoslovakia, and the French, together with the Russians, reaffirmed promises of immediate aid to the Czechs if they were attacked. Hitler was forced to back down, but only temporarily because the British now decided to assist him.

Some people in Britain felt that the Versailles settlement had been unfair and that it should be revised. The British Prime Minister, Neville Chamberlain, also agreed that the Germans had very strong ties with the Sudeten Germans. He decided that he could not lead his country into a general war to preserve Czech rule over a German minority, particularly as the British armed forces were still weak. As the tension between Germany and Czechoslovakia mounted through the summer, he took it upon himself to find a solution to the crisis, flying to Munich to meet Hitler at Berchtesgaden on September 15. He was easily convinced that Hitler would be satisfied, once he had gained the Sudetenland from Czechoslovakia.

The Munich Agreement

In his eagerness to avoid war, Chamberlain persuaded the French to support him and threatened to abandon the Czechs unless they gave up the Sudetenland. With reluctant Czech agreement to this, he flew back to Germany on September 22 to meet Hitler at Godesberg. He offered Hitler a peaceful transfer of all parts of the Sudetenland that were 50 per cent German-speaking, but this was not enough. The German leader demanded the whole of the Sudetenland. The Czech government refused.

Chamberlain was untiring in his efforts to meet German demands. He believed that if the wrongs done to Germany at Versailles were righted, then Germany would be "appeased" and become a satisfied, peaceful nation. He organized a Four-Power Conference at Munich on September 29, between Germany, Italy, France and Britain. At the Conference Hitler persisted with his demands and the other powers agreed to them. The Czechs were not represented.

Chamberlain returned to London claiming that he had secured "peace in our time" and the Czechs were informed of the Four-Power Agreement. They had no choice but to comply. The loss of the Sudetenland proved a fatal blow that precipitated the disintegration of the Czechoslovak state. In October the Poles seized a disputed area of Teschen, and in November Hungary took a long strip of border country. In early 1939, the Slovaks and the Ruthenes declared their independence from the Czechs. Always ready to take an advantage, Hitler intervened again. He summoned the Czech President, Emil Hacha, to Berlin and browbeat him into asking for a German protectorate over the remains of his state. On March 15, German troops marched into Bohemia and Moravia while the Hungarians occupied Ruthenia.

The failure of appeasement

This deliberate establishment of German government over a non-German people exhausted any goodwill that the British felt for German demands. Chamberlain's policy of appeasement was totally discredited. Until that moment Hitler seemed to have played his cards extraordinarily well and to have achieved momentous advantages without resorting to war.

Although the French had the more powerful army of the two Western Powers, they were not resolute enough to face Germany without British support. This support had been withheld while the British thought Hitler was a reasonable man. Once Chamberlain had been humiliated and German ambitions seemed unreasonable, the British were, at last, forced to accept the prospect of war as necessary to stop Europe falling under Axis control.

Neville Chamberlain returns from Munich, September 1938, announcing "peace in our time."

Britain tries to protect Poland

When the Germans began turning their attentions to Poland, another country that had been awarded German territory and people at Versailles, the British responded in March 1939 by introducing peacetime conscription, issuing gas masks to the civilian population, organizing the construction of air-raid shelters and mobilizing industry to manufacture war materiel. Chamberlain also announced that he would come to the aid of the Poles if they were attacked. There was, of course, not much that Britain could do without Russian or French help. In fact the Russians had lost confidence in the Western Allies, since their offer of help to the Czechs had been rejected.

British support may indeed have been positively unhelpful to the Poles. Hitler had made a non-aggression pact with Poland in 1934 and the two countries had been almost in the position of allies over the partition of Czechoslovakia.

The first German demands of the Poles did not seem unreasonable. Hitler wished to regain the German port of Danzig and the coastal corridor of land, which separated East Prussia from the rest of Germany. This would have denied the Poles their port of Gdynia and coastline, but Hitler hinted that they could be compensated at the expense of Russia and offered a firm alliance, which would include Poland in the Anti-Comintern Pact. All this was rejected by the Poles, who were probably over-confident because of their British alliance.

March and April of 1939 were bad months for the Western Powers. In March, Hitler demanded the return of the town of Memel from Lithuania; the Lithuanians had no choice but to comply. On April 1, Franco announced the final victory of the Fascists in Spain. Mussolini, intent upon carving out a Balkan empire, invaded Albania with 100,000 Italian troops. On May 22, Mussolini and Hitler signed the "Pact of Steel," which committed them to fight together in any war. To counterbalance this, the British and French started negotiating with the Soviet Union, but mutual suspicion prevented this from getting off the ground.

The Nazi-Soviet Pact

The tension increased throughout the summer until, in August, Stalin made a sudden diplomatic and military move designed to keep the Soviet Union out of the approaching war. He signed a pact of neutrality with Germany which pledged each country to remain neutral if the other was involved in a war. Stalin also forced a similar pact upon Germany's ally, Japan, after a remarkable military action.

A large Japanese force had crossed into Soviet Mongolia by the Khalkhin-Gol River. The local Soviet commander, General Georgi Zhukov, assembled an overwhelming force in great secrecy and used tanks and aircraft to surround and destroy the Japanese in eleven days, inflicting over 50,000 casualties. It was a remarkable military display, matched only by that of German forces in the next few days in Poland.

The Soviet pact with Hitler sealed Poland's fate. Hitler felt confident that his army could defeat the Poles very rapidly if they did not have Soviet support. He was freed from the fear of a war on two fronts – with the Soviet Union in the east and the democracies in the west. Because he was in such a strong position he may have believed that the democracies would back down and withdraw their support from Poland.

The German invasion of Poland

Hitler now decided to resolve the Polish crisis by force. He prepared his forces to attack Poland on September 1. By this time it was very unlikely that his quarrel with the Poles could be resolved peacefully, even if he was given all he had asked for. His military plans would proceed whatever happened, but there was still some slim hope that the British and French might abandon the Poles to their fate.

General Zhukov, Russia's greatest military commander in the Second World War, briefs soldiers during the fighting on the Khalkhin-Gol River, 1939.

Indeed, the long list of German successes – rearmament, the Rhineland, the *Anschluss*, Czechoslovakia – which had met with indecision from the Western Powers, seemed to indicate that they would only respond if their own territory was attacked. In fact the process of allowing Germany to recover from the settlement forced on her by Versailles had come to an end. Belatedly the democracies had realized that the Nazi regime was not only concerned with achieving a fair readjustment of the settlement but had a vaster, more unlimited ambition.

The democracies decided to make their stand over Poland. The German armies invaded Poland on September 1. Hitler was presented with a Franco-British ultimatum that, unless his forces withdrew, they would declare war on Germany. Hitler refused to halt his campaign and, on September 3, the Second World War began. France and Britain were once again at war with Germany.

Was war inevitable?

In a sense war had been inevitable ever since Hitler had come to power in 1933. Before its defeat in the First World War, Germany had been militarily Europe's most powerful nation. The size of the German population and industrial potential meant that Germany would resume its position as the most important power on the Continent, unless some restraints were imposed. The settlement of Versailles had tried to do this but it had been against the will of the German people. Hitler and, indeed, all German nationalists were determined that Germany should recover the position it had enjoyed before the Allies had defeated it. Only France saw the need to maintain German weakness and the French could expect support only from Britain, if at all, because their most powerful ally the United States – had withdrawn into isolationism.

German resurgence was probably inevitable. Under a different leader it might have occurred without provoking a general war but, under Hitler, an opportunist, it happened so quickly and so alarmingly that the British and French had to make a stand against it. An even greater tragedy lay in the future as a result of some of Hitler's aims, which were probably not widely understood by the Germans who voted for him so confidently in plebiscites. He would not be content with revenge for Versailles, but wanted to make his race the master of all others and to exterminate the Jews, whom he imagined to be the enemies of that purpose. The world was about to enter a new nightmare.

Refugees from Europe, fearful of Nazi Germany, flood into the United States during the 1930s.

CONFLICT IN THE 20TH CENTURY: APPENDICES

The period 1919-39 was a time of great political and economic upheavals which eventually led to the Second World War. This is strikingly illustrated by the contrast between the powerful personalities of the dictators and the rather weaker leaders who opposed them. The dictatorships all had private armies to help secure power; these were a common feature of the times. At the same time the course of the Second World War was being laid down by the great changes in the weapons and methods of warfare that were taking place.

PERSONALITIES

Leon Blum (1872-1950) three times Prime Minister of France (1936-37, 1938 and 1946-47). His first government, known as the Popular Front, instituted sweeping socialist reforms. After the fall of France in 1940, he was imprisoned until the end of the war.

Arthur Neville Chamberlain (1869-1940) became Prime Minister of Great Britain in 1937 and was the architect of the policy of appeasing Germany to avoid war. The invasion of Czechoslovakia in 1939 forced him to recognize that appeasement was impossible, as German demands were limitless. In September that year, he took Britain to war against Germany in response to the German invasion of Poland. His ineffective direction of the war led him to resign as Prime Minister in May 1940.

Chiang Kai-shek (1887-1975). Chinese Nationalist leader. He was a successful military commander of the Kuomintang (Chinese Nationalist Party) in its campaigns against the warlords who ruled parts of China. He became leader of the Kuomintang in 1925 and turned against its Communist allies in 1927. When the Japanese invaded China in 1931, the Kuomintang and the Communists reformed an uneasy alliance to face the common foe. Following Japan's defeat civil war broke out again in 1946 and the Communists succeeded in driving Chiang's forces out of mainland China by the end of 1949. Chiang set up the Republic of China on the island of Taiwan, which he ruled until his death.

Francisco Franco (1892-1975) Spanish dictator. He pursued a military career from the age of 14 and by 1935 was Chief of the General Staff. The following year he led a revolt against the Republican government that began the Spanish Civil War. After his victory over the Republicans in 1939, he became the autocratic ruler of Spain. His country achieved considerable economic advance during the last 20 years of his rule and he allowed a slight liberalization in the final months of his life, which enabled his

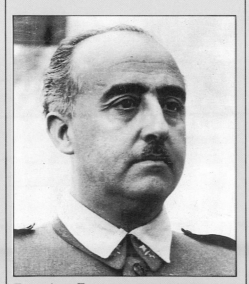

Francisco Franco

regime to be succeeded by a constitutional monarchy.

Adolf Hitler (1889-1945) German dictator. Born in Austria, he served in a Bavarian regiment as a corporal during the First World War. He became leader of the National Socialist (Nazi) German Workers' Party in 1921 and began a long, often violent, political campaign, aimed at seizing supreme power. He succeeded in 1933. Once in power he crushed his opponents, began his persecution of the Jews and launched a massive rearmament program in preparation for his wars of conquest. At first his forces enjoyed great military success but the tide of war turned against them in 1943. In April 1945, he committed suicide rather than face capture.

Kemal Ataturk (1881-1938) the founder of modern Turkey. He had been a distinguished general in the First World War and opposed the peace terms imposed after Turkey's defeat. In order to repudiate them, he deposed the Sultan and became President in 1923. From that date until his death, he introduced a series of reforms aimed at turning Turkey into a modern, secular and industrialized state.

Vladimir Ilyich Lenin (1870-1924) Russian revolutionary and leader of the Bolshevik party. Born Vladimir Ilyich Ulanov, he was in exile in Switzerland when the first World War began. He traveled back to Russia in secret once the revolution broke out in March 1917. He seized power in the second revolution of

November 1917, and agreed to an armistice with the Central Powers. As Chairman of the Communist Party, 1919-1924, he was virtual dictator of Russia.

Benito Mussolini (1883-1945) Italian dictator. He formed the *Fasci di Combattimento* in 1919. They wore a blackshirt uniform and used violence as a political weapon to bring Mussolini to power in 1922. His grandiose program of public works and expansionist foreign policy (typified by his invasion of Ethiopia in 1935) were popular. His decision to declare war on France and Britain in 1940 led his country into a string of military disasters. Increasingly unpopular, he was overthrown in 1943. His German allies then set him up as a puppet ruler of Northern Italy but their impending defeat left him powerless. He was hanged by Italian partisans in April 1945.

Franklin Delano Roosevelt (1882-1945) the only president to be elected to four terms. He pursued his political career despite being partially paralyzed from the waist down by poliomyelitis in 1921. He introduced the economic policies of the New Deal to relieve the effects of the Depression after his election in 1932. He attempted to keep the USA out of the Second World War but assisted the Western Allies in every

Benito Mussolini

way short of armed support, until the Japanese attack on the US fleet at Pearl Harbor in 1941, which brought the USA into the war. Roosevelt played a major part in deciding the strategy and policies of the Allies before his death in office shortly before final victory.

Joseph Stalin (1879-1953) Russian dictator. Born Iosif Dzhugashvili, he changed his name to Stalin after becoming a Marxist in the 1890s. In 1901 he joined what would become the Bolshevik Party. In 1902 he was imprisoned and then exiled for revolutionary activity. After the

Communists had taken control of Russia in 1917, he gained influence within the party leadership and became General Secretary of the Communist Party in 1922. After Lenin's death in 1924, he succeeded in eliminating all rivals for supreme power by 1929. He then instituted a program of industrial and agricultural modernization, as well as a reign of terror which tightened his control over the Soviet Union. In 1941 he took charge of the army and eventually led his country to victory over the Nazis in 1945. He maintained an attitude of unremitting hostility towards the Western democracies from the end of the Second World War until his death.

Lev Trotsky (1879-1940) founder of the Red Army. Born Lev Davidovitch Bronstein, he became a Marxist in the 1890s and was imprisoned and then exiled on two occasions. He played a prominent part in the October Revolution that brought the Bolsheviks to power. He became War Commissar in the Civil War (1918-20) and raised and led the Red Army to eventual victory. An intellectual and theorist, he was regarded as Lenin's natural successor but was outmaneuvered in a power struggle with Stalin. He was banished from the Soviet Union in 1929 and settled in Mexico, where he was murdered by Stalin's agents.

Vladimir Ilyich Lenin

Franklin Delano Roosevelt

Joseph Stalin

MAJOR POWERS

France

The Third Republic of France was a democracy, which did not work well because there were too many different parties represented in parliament. The world economic scene also affected the political climate considerably. During the first few years after 1918, the French faced the enormous financial outlay of rebuilding those parts of French territory that had been devastated by war. By the end of the 1920s there was growing and impressive prosperity but this was ended by the Depression. The economic difficulties of the 1930s polarized political differences: there were strong Fascist and Communist movements. There was little political continuity as governments, created from many parties in temporary alliances, rarely lasted long. On paper France was a great military power with a more powerful army than Germany. However the country had a defensive psychology and strongly fortified its north-eastern frontier. In addition, the politicians were unwilling to do much without British support. France was also a great colonial power which still demonstrated expansionist ambitions in Morocco.

Great Britain

Even British democracy had its troubles between the wars. In the early 1920s there was much unemployment and labor unrest. The country's first socialist government only lasted from January to November 1924 and was brought down largely by the intrigues of the right-wing press. In 1926 a Conservative government faced a General Strike, which was defeated but left a legacy of class bitterness. The impact of the Depression destroyed a second socialist government, which gave way to a National Government in 1931. A

The British Army was used to maintain law and order during the General Strike.

steady climb out of economic recession followed, but financial constraints made Britain slow to rearm in response to Hitler's aggressive foreign policy. Although still very much a great power, Britain no longer had absolute naval supremacy: she could be matched by the USA and even threatened by Japan. The British Army was largely a force designed to protect and police a great empire, although the socialist government recognized in the Statute of Westminster of 1931 that parts of that empire would be independent in the future.

Germany

The desperate hardship that followed defeat in the First World War disguised the fact that Germany could not be kept weak and disarmed for ever. However the early 1920s, under a weak democratic government, were a disastrous time, with the occupation of the Ruhr by the French, an interlude of raging inflation and a deep sense of national humiliation. The Locarno Treaties of 1925 reinstated Germany in the community of nations and began a period of prosperity under the chancellorship of Stresemann.

Germans transport paper money during the 1923 inflation crisis.

This ended when the Depression of 1929 brought an unemployment crisis. Years of political turmoil ended with the emergence of Hitler as a dictator in 1933. He instituted a rearmament program and expansion at the expense of Germany's neighbors. Germany acquired Italy and Japan as allies by November 1937 and during the next two years showed increasing hostility to France and Britain.

Italy

None of the political parties was strong enough to make Italy's fragile democracy work after 1918. A period of increasing disorder became worse after Mussolini formed his first government following the Fascist March on Rome in 1922, but he soon crushed all opposition and emerged as unquestioned dictator in 1924. He allowed the monarchy to remain and cultivated good relations with the Papacy and Roman Catholic Church to increase his popularity. Italy was not in reality a great power, but Mussolini's regime gave a false impression of strength and dynamism. As a result, Italy was wooed by France and Britain to help contain Germany. At first Mussolini responded and, as late as April 1935, the Stresa Conference demonstrated that Italy was in the anti-German camp. A complete change ensued following the rift caused between Italy and her former allies by the Ethiopian War in 1935. In November 1936 Mussolini proclaimed the Rome-Berlin Axis, which allied Italy firmly to Germany.

Japan

Ruled by a Divine Emperor whose will was sacrosanct in theory, government was in fact carried on by ministers appointed by the Emperor. Until 1926 a certain parliamentary liberalism was encouraged but, after that, the Emperor's autocratic powers were used by army leaders and extreme nationalists to form a militaristic dictatorship. In 1921 Japan's traditional alliance with Britain was dropped. Ten years later, Japan's attack on Manchuria

foreshadowed Japanese withdrawal from the League of Nations in 1933. This led to a deterioration of relations with the democratic powers that became worse after Japan's attack on China in 1937. Looking around for other allies, the Japanese rulers identified with Germany and Italy in the Anti-Comintern Pact of November 1936. The only other great power with strong land forces in the Far East was the Soviet Union, which signed a non-aggression pact with Japan in 1941.

Union of Soviet Socialist Republics

Between 1918 and 1920, the Communist government of the Soviet Union fought and won a bitter civil war against anti-Communist forces. Once established in government, the Communists led by Lenin found it difficult to win international recognition until the 1922 Rapallo Treaty with Germany ended diplomatic isolation. Lenin died in 1924 and Stalin emerged as undisputed dictator five years later. Stalin was very concerned to build up the industrial and military power of the Soviet Union, so that any attack by anti-Communist powers could be resisted. It was in order to buy time for this build-up that the Russians intervened on the Republican side in Spain in 1936 – they hoped to keep the Fascist

powers embroiled there. For the same reason the Russians hoped for an alliance with the democracies against Nazi Germany, but despaired of French and British inactivity after the Nazi invasion of Czechoslovakia. To gain a slice of Polish territory and to buy off the Nazi threat, the Soviet Union negotiated a non-aggression pact with Germany in August 1939.

United States of America

Easily the richest nation in the world and therefore a potential superpower, the United States dropped all interest in foreign affairs almost as soon as the First World War ended. Congress refused to ratify the Treaty of Versailles and America then dissociated itself from the League of Nations and never became a member. The country concentrated on economic growth throughout the 1920s in a very conservative political atmosphere which even saw the nationwide introduction of Prohibition in 1920. A series of Republican Presidents held power during this time, but the Stock Market Crash of October 1929 ushered in the economic Depression that was to dominate American life and politics throughout the 1930s. A Democratic President, Roosevelt, was elected in 1932. He introduced the more liberal economic policies of the New Deal and ended Prohibition, effective January 1934.

US policemen round up illicit drinkers during Prohibition.

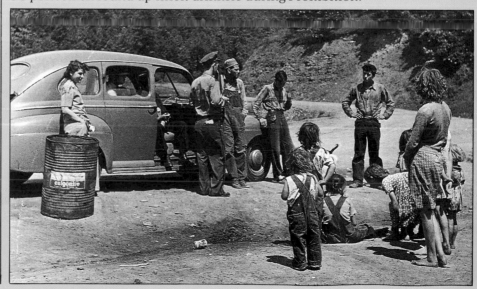

PRIVATE ARMIES

In the immediate aftermath of the First World War, the politics of many European countries veered towards the extreme. The apparent success of the Bolshevik revolution in Russia led to the widespread formation of Communist parties and, in certain cases, to attempted insurrections on the Russian model, notably in Germany in 1918 and 1919. In response, right-wing political groups sprang up, dedicated to the preservation of the state, the destruction of left-wing socialist and Communist movements and the imposition of strongly nationalistic, totalitarian regimes.

Usually taken together under the term "Fascists," these groups varied in organization and detailed aims from country to country. A common denominator was their dependence, in the early stages of their growth, on "private armies" of thugs and activists who were prepared to go onto the streets to intimidate their opponents. The objective was to create a "climate of collapse," which would help the group seize political power. As left-wing groups also raised private armies, street fights became depressingly common.

Italy

The process began in Italy where, as early as 1919, the poet Gabriele d'Annunzio formed an ex-servicemen's organization known as the *Arditi* ("Children of God") to oppose the Communists. They were the first to use the raised arm salute and were distinctive in their paramilitary uniforms. However the *Arditi* were soon overshadowed by Benito Mussolini's *Fasci di Combattimento*. They were the first of the political private armies and their "Black Shirts" were active in the suppression of riots, strikes and factory sit-ins between 1920 and 1922. Deliberately projected as upholders of law and order, the

Members of the Italian youth movement, the ~~Balilla~~, on parade. Giovane italiane

Fasci ("groups") spearheaded Mussolini's successful "March on Rome" in 1922. Once in power Mussolini, *Il Duce* ("the leader"), maintained the Fascist organization and used it to dominate Italian politics down to the lowest levels. He even created a special youth movement – the *Balilla.*(boys)

Germany

A similar development occurred in Germany, where right-wing Freikorps ("Free Corps") emerged in 1919 in response to the left-wing Spartacist Rising in Berlin. Composed mainly of ex-army officers, the *Freikorps* were strongly nationalistic, dedicated to the elimination of "traitors to the Fatherland," and most members continued to wear their army uniforms. Their influence was undermined in 1923 with the recreation of a German Army (the *Reichswehr*), but many ex-*Freikorps*

German SA units shortly before the "Night of the Long Knives."

members, expressing the widespread sense of betrayal at the terms of the 1919 peace settlement, went on to join the Nazi Party and its private army – the *Sturm Abteilungen* ("storm troops") or SA.

Founded by Major Ernst Roehm, the SA, distinctive in its brown shirts and swastika arm-bands, acted as the strong-arm element of the Nazis. They disrupted left-wing meetings, intimidated anyone who did not support their views, attacked the Jews (who were blamed for Germany's weakness) and fought rival groups in the streets. By 1933, the SA could boast 2.3 million members and it was so strong that Hitler feared it as a political rival.

However, Hitler had prepared for its destruction. In 1929 he had authorized Heinrich Himmler to raise a group of dedicated Nazis, known as the *Schütz Staffeln* ("Protection Detachments") or SS. Dressed in black with death's-head insignia, the SS gradually increased its strength until, on June 30, 1934, it was used to counter the SA. In the "Night of the Long Knives," Roehm and over 70 of his key followers were arrested and executed, paving the way to the development of the SS as one of the most feared organizations in modern history.

Britain
But it was not just the Fascists and Nazis who raised right-wing political armies. In Britain, the Imperial Fascist League had emerged in the 1920s under the leadership of Arnold Spencer Leese, and in October 1932 Sir Oswald Mosley created the British Union of Fascists (BUF) in direct opposition to socialist groups.

The BUF, with its black-shirted activists and "bolt-of-lightning" badge, used the familiar tactics of beating up its opponents, disrupting rival political meetings and intimidating Jews, but it did not enjoy a great deal of success. By 1936, the government had banned the wearing of political uniforms in public and Mosley had lost popular support by openly advocating an alliance with Hitler. By 1939, the BUF had virtually ceased to exist.

Spain
More success was enjoyed by the *Falange* party in Spain, also founded in 1932. Initially, its appeal was relatively small – under the leadership of José Antonio Primo de Rivera, it mustered only 8,000 members by 1935 – but its association with Francisco Franco's Nationalists in the Civil War ensured its lasting influence.

Dressed in blue shirts with the Yoke and Arrow badge of Catholic Spain on a red and gold flag of revolution, the *Falange* enjoyed the fruits of political power after 1939. They are still active in Spanish politics today, suitably muted. In 1941, the *Falange* sponsored the raising of a special Blue Division to join the Germans on the Eastern Front against the Soviets.

France
In France, too, the Fascists gained some political ground, although the number of different groups made their influence less than it might have been. As early as 1919, *Action Française* emerged as an anti-Communist organization, giving rise later to the *Comité Secret d'Action Révolutionnaire* (CSAR), whose members were known as *Cagoulards* ("Hooded Men") because of their secrecy.

They were rivaled on the right wing by groups which included Pierre Taittinger's *Jeunesses Patriotes* (in blue raincoats and berets) and the popular *Croix de Feu*, and they opposed a host of left-wing forces which included Jacques Doriot's *Parti Populaire Français*.

Other countries
Elsewhere, the private armies enjoyed mixed fortunes. In Eastern Europe, the Legion of the Archangel Michael, or "Iron Guard," was influential in Rumania and the Arrow Cross was active in the politics of Hungary.

In Belgium, the *Rex* Party of Léon Degrelle appeared and in the United States the German-American *Bund*, based in New York, modeled itself on the Nazi Party.

But it was in Italy and Germany that the private armies of the right flourished.

Sir Oswald Mosley at a British Union of Fascists rally in London, 1934.

LAND WARFARE

There was a vast difference between the conduct of military operations in the First and Second World Wars. The First was characterized by a static trench deadlock in which huge armies outran their supplies the minute they left the essential railheads too far behind them. In the Second there were fast-moving and decisive battles fought between armored fighting vehicles, supported by fully mechanized units, often supplied by trucks.

Throughout the First World War the air weapon was in its infancy but, in the Second, it had developed a terrifying power of ground attack to help the armored spearheads of the ground forces cut through opposition. It also brought civilians into the battle zone as fleets of heavy bombers razed great cities.

At sea too there was a change: in the First World War, the major engagements had been fought between gun-armed, ironclad battleships, but in the Second, the important fleet actions were decided by carrier-borne aircraft.

Tank development

Many military developments occurred in the period between the two world wars. The most striking of them was the use of armored and mechanized ground formations which, for various reasons, could only be operated effectively by the Germans in the first years of the war.

The principal weapon used in this new type of warfare was the tank. Some Germans, such as Hans von Seeckt and Heinz Guderian, gave much thought to tank design between the wars so, at first, they possessed an advantage in the quality of their equipment over some of their opponents. Yet this advantage was never very marked, nor was it universal. The Russians developed and used tanks which were far superior to anything available throughout the rest of the world by 1941.

Elsewhere, tank development received a low priority. In the United States, the Tank Corps was abolished in 1920 and existing tanks handed over to the infantry. In France, tanks were also used as auxiliary weapons by the infantry. In Britain it was a different story. The world's foremost thinkers on the new armored warfare and the "expanding torrent of armor" that would engulf the battlefields of future wars were British – Major-General J F C Fuller and Captain Basil Liddell Hart.

This meant that British tank specialists had some idea what to expect from the new tactics that came to be called *Blitzkrieg*. Their ideas, however, found little favor with politicians and some senior soldiers. As a result the Experimental Mechanized Force, founded in 1927, was abolished in 1929. Only in Germany were the new ideas adopted, even though the German High Command was very much against them.

German tanks

After the First World War, no one had any real idea about the operational requirements of tank forces or of the future importance of the Main Battle Tank (MBT). This incorporated in a single vehicle the best possible combination of firepower, maneuverability and protection.

As a result, it was common

The Panzer III was a great improvement on the Panzers I and II and entered service in 1939.

The Vickers Medium tank Mk II was Britain's standard tank between the wars.

practice to produce three tank types – heavy, medium and light – so that some part of the armored force could adopt a fast-moving role, while others could assist deliberate attacks on defended positions.

Even the Germans fell victim to this uncertainty and put different tank types into production in the 1930s – Panzers I, II, III and IV. Panzers I and II were designed as training tanks. They were too light and underprotected, so that by 1939 they were recognized as out of date. The Panzers III and IV were to prove reasonable vehicles until 1941-42, when they were overtaken by better models, the Panzer V "Panther" and Panzer VI "Tiger."

The original Panzer IV produced during the 1930s had armor only 30mm thick and a 37 or 75-mm gun of low velocity and poor armor-piercing power. It also had an unimpressive top speed of 32km/h (20 mph). It was not too bad a weapons system by the standards of the 1930s but it could be matched by the French and Russians.

Italian and British tanks

The Italians formed a large armored regiment in 1927, equipped with light, fast tanks which were also highly vulnerable. These were Fiats which had a mere 13mm of armored protection and had no main gun armament, only two machine guns. In December 1935, a squadron of Italian light tanks was destroyed and the crews killed by Ethiopian tribesmen armed with swords and old-fashioned rifles at a gorge on the Takkaze River. They were to prove even less useful against better-armed enemies.

One of these enemies was the British Army, which formed its first armored division in 1939. Although its tanks were better than the Italians', it did not have vehicles to rival the Panzer III and IV. The British armored force comprised mainly light and cruiser tanks. The heavy tanks were designed for infantry support and had a top speed little faster than walking.

The light tanks had two machine guns but the cruisers had much more formidable armament: some had a 2-pounder gun with two machine guns, while others had three machine guns to go with a 2-pounder or a 3.7-inch mortar. Unfortunately all the light and cruiser tanks had such thin armor that they could be knocked out very easily.

French and Russian tanks

During the 1930s, the French and Russians produced tanks which had the greatest potential for armored warfare. The best French tanks had 60-mm armor, a 75-mm gun and a top speed of 40km/h (25 mph).

By 1940, the Russian High Command was already evaluating prototypes of the T-34 tank, which was to be considered the finest all-around armored fighting vehicle of the Second World War. It had armor up to 45mm thick, a 76-mm main gun backed up by two machine guns and a maximum speed of 55km/h (34 mph). When it appeared in June 1941, it was superior to anything the Germans had had available for several years.

Outside Europe, only the United States was producing tanks, but not in any quantity.

Blitzkrieg tactics

Although German tank design was not absolutely superior, the German Army was able to produce an unbroken string of victories for three years (1939-42) because it was the only army which had adopted the British concept of mobile warfare and the penetration of an enemy front by an "expanding torrent of armor."

The German secret was in the formation of Panzer divisions – mechanized formations in which the infantry, artillery, workshops and supply units could keep pace with a strong tank force as it broke through an enemy front and then raced at bewildering speed through the enemy's rear areas to confuse and encircle enemy fighting troops.

These Panzer divisions were not dispersed but kept together as a concentrated strike force to make and exploit the decisive breach. This concept was equally well understood by the Soviet Marshal Mikhail Tukhachevski, who created Russian tank corps which were the equal of the German Panzers. In May 1937, Stalin ordered Tukhachevski arrested and shot. After this the tank corps was broken up.

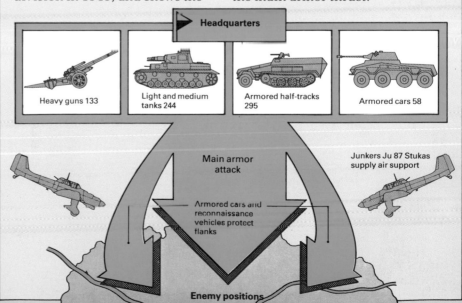

Blitzkrieg in action
This diagram is based on the actions of a single Panzer division in 1940, and shows the main elements of Blitzkrieg. As reconnaissance units probe forward, Ju 87s blast open gaps for the main armor thrust.

Headquarters

Heavy guns 133

Light and medium tanks 244

Armored half-tracks 295

Armored cars 58

Main armor attack

Junkers Ju 87 Stukas supply air support

Armored cars and reconnaissance vehicles protect flanks

Enemy positions

AIR WARFARE

Dive-bombers

Besides their organization of the Panzer divisions, the Germans enjoyed another crucial advantage: the development of close support from ground-attack aircraft. In the First World War aircraft had usually been constructed of wood braced with wires but during the 1920s these gave way to a new breed of monoplane aircraft covered in metal. Better streamlining and more powerful engines produced much faster planes which were highly maneuverable.

In America and Germany there was great interest in dive-bombers, which could be devastatingly accurate. The basic German dive-bomber developed was the Junkers Ju 87, called the "Stuka." It was used to great effect in the Spanish Civil War and later played a crucial part as "flying artillery" in the success of the Panzer divisions.

The Americans also had a number of interesting dive-bomber types in service or design in the 1930s and their successors were to play a vital role in the Navy's victories in the Pacific after 1942.

Bombers

Dive-bombers were designed to be used in a tactical role as close support to ground formations, but larger bombers were also developed for a strategic role. Nearly all the powers had a number of medium bomber types which could also double as transport aircraft, as the German Junkers Ju 52s showed so successfully when they transported Franco's Army of North Africa to Spain in 1936.

These medium bombers could carry a deadly enough payload of bombs to threaten whole cities, but they were eclipsed in their destructive potential by the heavy bombers being developed in Britain and the United States. In the US the

Ju 87 "Stuka," fitted with sirens to terrify victims of its dive-bombing.

designs for the Boeing B-17 Flying Fortress and the Consolidated B-24 Liberator had materialized by the end of the 1930s and both aircraft would prove capable of carrying 3,600kg (7,950lb) of bombs.

By this time the British had also produced designs for their formidable four-engined heavy bombers, such as the Short Stirling, which were to raze German cities in their strategic bombing offensive.

Nothing was more significant to the British than this development of

heavy bombers. British confidence that mass strategic bombing of whole areas would prove a decisive weapon was only matched by British fear of the sort of war this would entail. The RAF chiefs were firm in their belief in the theories of strategic bombing, propounded by such people as the Italian Giulio Douhet and the American Billy Mitchell. They were convinced that there was no effective defense against bombers intent on the destruction of industries and

Boeing B-17 Flying Fortress

Polikarpov I-16

The Bf 109 had British contemporaries that were to prove its equal in the Hawker Hurricane and Supermarine Spitfire. The Americans were also building a similar machine in the Curtiss P-40.

Carrier-borne aircraft

This concentration on air power was not confined to land forces and the Americans and Japanese also grasped its importance at sea. All three of the world's great naval powers had put aircraft carriers into service during the 1930s, but the British had taken little trouble to produce maritime aircraft types, although their biplane Fairey Swordfish torpedo bomber gave them surprisingly good service.

In contrast the Japanese developed the Mitsubishi A6M "Zero" fighter which performed to the standard of most land-based fighters. This was almost matched by the US Navy's Grumman F4F Wildcat.

This extension of seapower into three dimensions (for the submarine had taken it below the waves as early as the First World War) was to have a profound effect on naval thinking. In fleet actions between first-class powers, the aircraft carrier was to prove far more valuable than the ironclad battleships.

civilian centers. Their advice bred the fear that war would be unimaginably destructive in the minds of British politicians. That helped to create the policy of avoiding war by appeasement.

Fighters

This fear of the bomber was exaggerated and one of the reasons for that was that fighter interceptors were also being successfully developed during the 1930s. These had two tasks: to defend the homeland against the bomber and to gain air superiority over the battlefield. At first, the Russians led the world in this field with the Polikarpov I-16, which had a semi-enclosed cockpit, retractable undercarriage and cannon as well as machine-gun armament. Fighters of this type enjoyed great initial success in the Spanish Civil War, but their radial engines gave them less power than the in-line engines of the German Messerschmitt Bf 109s that swept them from the skies.

Hawker Hurricane

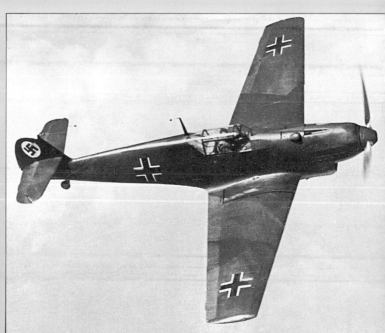

Messerschmitt Bf 109

CHRONOLOGY

1918

October 28 Naval mutinies begin in Kiel, Germany

November 11 Armistice on the Western Front

1919

January 5-11 Spartacist rising in Berlin crushed by *Freikorps*

January 18 Paris Peace Conference opens

February 14 League of Nations Covenant approved

March 4 Comintern founded in Moscow

June 21 Kemal issues Turkish Declaration of Independence

June 28 Versailles Treaty signed

September 10 St Germain Treaty signed

November 27 Neuilly Treaty signed

1920

January 1 Prohibition in force in the USA

March 13 Kapp Putsch in Berlin

April 25 Polish offensive against Russia begins

June 4 Treaty of Trianon signed

July 6 Russian offensive against Poles begins

August 10 Treaty of Sèvres accepted by the Turkish Sultan

1921

March 8-16 Lenin launches the New Economic Policy

March 18 Peace Treaty of Riga between Poland and Russia

November 12 Washington Conference opens

December 6 Agreement between Britain and Irish Nationalists sets up Irish Free State

1922

April 16 Treaty of Rapallo between Germany and Russia

August 26-September 9 Turks defeat Greeks at Smyrna, Asia Minor

September 23 Chanak crisis sees a confrontation between British and Turkish troops

October 28 Mussolini's march on Rome succeeds

1923

January 11-12 Occupation of the Ruhr by French troops begins

April 30 Irish Civil War ends in cease-fire

July 24 Treaty of Lausanne between Turkey, Greece and the Allies

August 2 US President Harding dies and Coolidge replaces him

October 29 Turkish Republic proclaimed with Kemal Ataturk as President

November 8-9 Hitler's Beer Hall Putsch fails

1924

January 21 Lenin dies

January 23 First Labor Government in Britain

April 1 Hitler sentenced to imprisonment

1925

January 16 Trotsky dismissed

from chairmanship of Russian Revolutionary Council

April 26 Hindenburg elected German President

August 27 French troops leave the Ruhr

December 1 Locarno Treaties signed

1926

April 24 German-Soviet non-aggression pact

May 4-12 British General Strike

September 10 Germany enters League of Nations

October 19 Trotsky expelled from Politburo

1928

April 23-29 Soviet Communist Party Congress adopts the First Five-Year Plan

August 27 Kellogg-Briand Pact signed

1929

January 31 Trotsky expelled from the Soviet Union

October 3 German Chancellor Stresemann dies

October 29 Stock Market Crash

1930

April 22 London Naval Treaty between Britain, USA and Japan

September 14 German *Reichstag* elections – Nazis win 107 seats and become the second largest party

1931

April 14 King Alfonso XIII leaves Spain and the Second Republic proclaimed in Spain

September 18 Mukden Incident leads to Japanese invasion of Manchuria

1932

January 22 Second Five-Year Plan begins in Soviet Union

January 28 Japanese and Chinese clash at Shanghai

March 9 Japan proclaims puppet state of Manchukuo (Manchuria)

April 10 Hindenburg defeats Hitler in German Presidential elections

June 16-July 9 Lausanne Conference agrees to end reparations

July 31 German Reichstag elections – Nazis win 230 seats

November 8 Roosevelt elected US President

1933

January 30 Hitler becomes German Chancellor

February 27 Reichstag Fire

March 4 Roosevelt becomes President – the New Deal is launched

March 23 Hitler secures Enabling Act to become dictator

March 27 Japan leaves League of Nations

October 14 Germany leaves League of Nations

December 5 Prohibition repealed in the USA

1934

June 29-30 Night of the Long Knives sees the destruction of the SA

August 2 Death of Hindenburg gives Hitler supreme power

September 18 Russia joins League of Nations

October 6 Armed uprising in Asturias, Spain

October 15 Chinese Communists begin the Long March

December 1 Assassination of Kirov leads to the purges in the Soviet Union

1935

January 13 Plebiscite in the Saar – vote for union with Germany

June 18 Anglo-German Naval Agreement signed

September 15 Nuremberg laws introduced – persecution of the Jews begins in earnest

October 3 Italians invade Ethiopia

October 19 League votes sanctions against Italy

October 20 End of the Chinese Communist Long March

1936

February 16 Popular Front wins Spanish elections

March 7 Germany re-occupies the Rhineland

May 9 Mussolini announces annexation of Ethiopia

June 4 Blum forms Popular Front Ministry in France

July 15 Sanctions against Italy end

July 17 Spanish Civil War begins

November 1 Mussolini announces Rome-Berlin Axis

November 25 Anti-Comintern Pact signed

1937

February 5-24 Spanish Nationalists defeated at Battle of Jarama

June 12 Soviet Army generals are purged

July 7 Sino-Japanese War begins

September 10-14 Nyon Conference held

October 19 Franco conquers northwest Spain

November 6 Italy joins the German-Japanese Anti-Comintern Pact

November 9 Japanese capture Shanghai

1938

February 4 German Army Commander-in-Chief Fritsch resigns

March 13 Anschluss proclaimed

September 29 Munich Agreement signed

October 1-10 Germany occupies Sudetenland

October 1 Poland occupies Teschen area of Czechoslovakia

November 2 Hungary occupies part of Czechoslovakia

1939

March 15 Germany annexes rest of Czechoslovakia

April 1 Franco announces end of Spanish Civil War

April 27 Britain introduces conscription

May 22 Germany and Italy announce Pact of Steel

August 20 Soviet victory over Japanese troops in Mongolia

August 23 Nazi-Soviet non-aggression pact signed

September 1 German invasion of Poland

September 3 Britain and France declare war on Germany

INDEX

Note: Numbers in bold refer to illustrations or maps

FURTHER READING

Bullock, Alan, *Hitler: A Study in Tyranny*, rev ed (Harper & Row, 1964)

Carsten, F L, *The Rise of Fascism*, 2nd ed (Berkeley: University of California Press, 1980)

Chaney, O P, *Zhukov* (Norman: University of Oklahoma Press, 1972)

Che Guevara, E, *Guerrilla Warfare* (Random House, 1968)

Cooper, Matthew, *The German Army 1933-45* (Zebra, 1979)

Detwiler, Donald S, *Germany, A Short History* (Carbondale, IL: Southern Illinois University Press, 1976)

Deutscher, Isaac, *Stalin: A Political Biography*, 2nd ed (Oxford University Press, 1952)

Hemingway, Ernest, *For Whom the Bell Tolls* (Scribners, 1940)

Hemingway, Ernest, *A Moveable Feast* (Scribners, 1964)

Hofstadter, Richard, *The American Political Tradition and the Men Who Made It*, 2nd ed (Knopf, 1973)

Howarth, Tony, *Twentieth Century History: The World since 1900* (Longman, 1979)

Isherwood, Christopher, "Goodbye to Berlin" in *The Berlin Stories* (New Directions, 1954)

Marks, Sally, *The Illusion of Peace: International Relations 1918-1933* (St Martin's, 1976)

Morton, Scott, *Japan: Its History and Culture* (McGraw-Hill 1984)

Orwell, George, *Homage to Catalonia* (Harcourt Brace, 1969)

Orwell, George, *The Road to Wigan Pier* (Harcourt Brace, 1972)

Peacock, H L, *Europe and Beyond, 1870 to 1976*, 2nd ed (Portsmouth, NH: Heinemann, 1977)

Robottom, John, *Modern China* (Longman 1978)

Rundle, R N, *International Affairs 1890-1939* (Holmes and Meier, 1980)

Steinbeck, John, *The Grapes of Wrath* (Viking, 1939)

Taylor, A J P, *The Origins of the Second World War* (Atheneum, 1983)

Thomas, Hugh, *The Spanish Civil War*, rev ed (Harper & Row, 1977)

Whalley, Stephen, Jr, *Mao Tse-tung: A Critical Biography* (Franklin Watts, 1975)

(NOTE: *All publishers located in New York unless specified otherwise*)

ACKNOWLEDGMENTS

Cover: MARS; page 5: Popperfoto; page 7: Popperfoto; page 8: Bundesarchiv, Koblenz; page 9: Bundesarchiv, Koblenz; page 11: Preussischer Kulturbesitz; pages 12-13: Ullstein Bilderdienst; page 13: Photosource/Keystone; page 14: Novosti; page 15: Novosti; page 17: Bundesarchiv, Koblenz; page 18 (left): Ullstein Bilderdienst; page 18 (right): E.T. Archive; page 19: Photosource/Keystone; page 20-21: Novosti; page 21: Novosti; page 22: Preussischer Kulturbesitz; page 24: MARS; page 25 (both): Bundesarchiv, Koblenz; pages 26-27: UPI/Bettman; page 28: Popperfoto; page 29: Popperfoto; page 31: Photosource/Fox; page 32: Photosource/Keystone; page 34: Photosource/Keystone; page 35 (top): Ediciones Urbion, Madrid; page 35 (bottom): Camera Press; page 36: Camera Press; page 37: Robert Hunt; page 38: MARS; page 39: Robert Hunt; page 40 (top): MARS; page 40 (bottom): Ullstein Bilderdienst; page 41: Suddeutscher Verlag; page 43: Preussischer Kulturbesitz; page 45: Photosource/Keystone; page 46: Robert Hunt; page 47: UPI/Bettman; page 48: Barnaby's; page 49 (top): Photosource/Keystone; page 49 (bottom left): Photosource/Central Press; page 49 (bottom center): Popperfoto; page 49 (bottom right): Photosource/Keystone; page 50 (top): Syndication International; page 50 (bottom): Bundesarchiv, Koblenz; page 51: Photosource; page 52 (top): Popperfoto; page 52 (bottom): Ullstein Bilderdienst; page 53: Photosource/Central Press; page 56 (top): Ullstein Bilderdienst; page 56 (bottom): James Gilbert; page 57 (top): Pilot Press; page 57 (bottom left): James Gilbert; page 57 (bottom right): Pilot Press.